GIANT JETLINERS

F-WWKU
071

Swire Group

First published in 1997 by Motorbooks International Publishers & Wholesalers, PO Box 1, 729 Prospect Avenue, Osceola, WI 54020-0001 USA

Motorbooks International books are also available at discounts in bulk quantity for industrial or sales-promotional use. For details write to Special Sales Manager at the Publisher's address

Library of Congress Cataloging-in-Publication Data Available

ISBN 0-7603-0373-8

On the front cover: Iran Air was one of the original customers for the 747SP and used the aircraft for its long-haul flight from Tehran to New York. This aircraft was one of the last to be delivered before the overthrow of the Shah in 1979 and was still being flown by the airline in the late 1990s.

On the back cover, top: Captain Hakata Atushiro fights a gusting 30-knot cross wind to bring his ANA 767-300 onto finals to Hong Kong's tricky approach to Runway 13 at Kai Tak International. Twenty seconds later and another flight from Japan's Kansai airport is successfully completed.

On the back cover, bottom: The DC-10 tail engine inlet is slightly oval with the inlet lips thickened on the side. This was designed to keep the flow of air into the inlet smooth even at the most severe condition, a high crosswind.

On the frontispiece: Western avionics and engines were used for the first time in the Il-96M. A suite of Rockwell Collins digital avionics gave the Russian jetliner's cockpit a distinctly Western feel. The display was dominated by six CRT displays, which showed navigation, primary flight, engine, and systems status in the usual way. Only the cyrillic characters of the Russian alphabet (named after the ninth century monk, St. Cyril), used on the panel and several controls, give away the aircraft's true origins.

On the title page: The new livery of Hong Kong-based Cathay Pacific was revealed for the first time in August 1994 as the airline's initial A330-300 was rolled out in Toulouse. Cathay launched the Rolls-Royce Trent 700 engine on the A330, making it the first Airbus to be powered by the British engine.

Edited by Mike Haenggi

Designed by Katie Finney

Printed in China through World Print, Ltd.

CONTENTS

ACKNOWLEDGMENTS

We are indebted to the many employees, past and present, of Airbus Industrie, Boeing, Lockheed Martin, McDonnell Douglas, Northrop Grumman, General Electric, Pratt & Whitney, and Rolls-Royce who have contributed information to make this book possible. We particularly wish to thank Adam Brown and David Velupillai of Airbus; Mike Bair, Susan Bradley, Phil Condit, John Hayhurst, Ida Hawkins, Duane Jackson, Tom Lubbesmeyer, Debbie Nomaguchi, Fred Solis, Joe Sutter, Chris Villiers, Doug Webb, and Tom Winfrey of Boeing. From Lockheed Martin we thank Elliott Green, Keith Mordorf, Jeff Rhodes, and Bob Slayman. Of the many McDonnell Douglas people who helped, we would like to thank Tom Downey, Don Hanson, Bob Saling, and Dale Warren. Thanks also to Mike Greywitt of Northrop Grumman, Rick Kennedy of General Electric, Robert Rosati and Mark Sullivan of Pratt & Whitney, Martin Brodie and Robert Nuttall of Rolls-Royce, and Alan Brown and Gordon Fullerton of NASA. For photographic assistance, we are indebted to the following: Captain Hakata Atushiro, John Bailey, Ed Baker, Tom Begley, John Braden, Austin Brown, Charles Cannon, Tony S. K. Chan, Chung Kim-Fung, Mark Challoner, Anthony Concil, Geoff Davies, Bo Draper, Bruce Drum, Pham Duong, Jerry Finch, William Fletcher, Kimberly Foster, Karen Friend, Richard Greener, Keith Harman, Dave Hughes, Allan Hurran, Chihiro Ishikawa, Captain Sadayoshi Ito, Kensuke Kotera, Hideki Kuroki, Jenny P. S. Lei, Captain Mike Livesley, Captain Ian Johnson, Steve Klodt, Andy Marsh, Eric McGahan, Ryuichi Mezaki, Yvonne Napper, Ken Nishikata, Captain Sueo Otsuka, Darren Roberts, Jim Reynolds, Hiroshi Sakatsume, Naoya Sato, Pat Schoneberger, Hiroshi Shimada, Captain Kazuhiko Shindo, Dick Siegel, Bryan Southgate, Tetsuhisa Sugano, Martin Taylor, Hideki Tezuka, Katsuhiko Tokunaga, Hernando Vergara, Katsuhiko Yumino, and Anthony Wong. For statistical assistance, we are grateful to Robert Grundy. Thanks also to the staff of Flight International, particularly Allan Winn, Max Kingsley-Jones, Graham Warwick, and Douglas Barrie. For support and proofreading, our thanks to Judy Norris, Lucy Bristow, and Melanie Wright, and to Anna Ravelo. A big thank you, as always, to our Motorbooks editor, Michael Haenggi.

Guy Norris and Mark Wagner

INTRODUCTION

Jumbo jets, wide-bodies, twin-aisles, multi-aisles, megajets, high-capacity transports—call them what you will, they are all giant jetliners. Today, their enormous presence is taken for granted, yet in less than 30 years these huge aircraft have completely transformed air transport and much of the world they serve.

The wide-body revolution of the early 1970s sparked a new era in mass transport from which world trade, travel, and the economy have never looked back. Thanks to much lower operating costs, the advent of the new giant jetliners meant travel was suddenly more affordable. People and goods began moving in unprecedented numbers. In 1957, when the jet-airliner age was only eight years old and giant jetliners were the stuff of fiction, some 90 million people traveled by air, twice as many as in 1952. In 1971, fewer than 200 wide-bodied jetliners had been delivered, yet the number of air travelers had mushroomed to 325 million. Less than a decade later this had grown to 750 million, and by 1997 almost 1.5 billion people were expected to make a journey by air.

While the impact of this new species of aircraft can be quantified in terms of passengers and profits, the wider-ranging effects of the air-transport revolution can only be guessed at. The new wide-bodies allowed an interchange of cultures, customs, and traditions at a speed and scale unparalleled in human history. Some believe this process has actually been destructive to many non-Western cultures. Others think the enormous exposure to different peoples has done more to promote peace and understanding over the past 30 years than any number of arms treaties and political settlements.

As Pan American president Juan Trippe said when taking delivery of the first wide-body jetliner, ". . . for 20 years the 747 will mean fast, low-cost means of transportation on a scale never before available for the traveling and shipping public at home and abroad . . . far more important than its effects on fares and rates, however, will be its effect on human society and human history. The new era of mass travel between nations may well prove more significant to human destiny than the atom bomb. The 747 will be a great weapon for peace."

In many ways, therefore, the wide-body revolution had as great an effect on world travel as the invention of ocean-going steamships in the early nineteenth century. Faraway places were no longer the sole preserve of the rich or the military. Travel was safer, cheaper, and more reliable.

Giant jetliners also had a major effect on the aerospace industry itself. The creation of these monstrous aircraft became almost a rite of passage for the few giant companies that dared to become involved. Most literally bet the company on the decision to go ahead with the fantastically expensive and risky technical venture of designing, developing, building, testing, and selling the giant jetliners. The risk was too much for some. Some airframe and engine companies were pushed into bankruptcy; others teetered on the brink of insolvency.

The road to today's wide-body fleet is littered with triumph and tragedy. Although bitter lessons were learned the hard way in terrible crashes, a far greater number of technical triumphs were achieved without lives being lost. While safety rightly comes under the microscope whenever a crash occurs, particularly of a wide-body, the overall improvements in air safety are often forgotten. The first generation of giant jetliners has an impressive safety record: the Lockheed L-1011 TriStar has a hull loss (or write-off) rate of only 0.77 per million take-

The world-shrinking impact of giant jetliners has transformed international trade and travel since the 1970s. Wide-bodied jets are set to play a vital part in keeping pace with mushrooming demand for air travel which is expected to grow by 70 percent worldwide through 2006. Here, one of the original breed, a TWA Boeing 747-100, coasts high over the Atlantic on yet another long-haul flight.

▼ Crowded ramps and ever-busier airspace were an accepted fact of life in many parts of the world by the mid-1990s. Hong Kong, which was handed back by the British to the Chinese in 1997, suffered its fair share but was expected to play a big part in the continuing surge in air travel in the region. By the end of the 1990s air travel in China alone was expected to grow at more than 14 percent per year compared to 4 percent for North America.

▲ Little and large. Booming air travel in Asia, and particularly in Japan, continues to drive the need for bigger jetliners. An ANA 747-400D (D for domestic) casts a mighty shadow at Tokyo's Haneda airport as a brand-new JAS McDonnell Douglas MD-90 scurries past in the background.

Captain Hakata Atushiro fights a gusting 30-knot cross wind to bring his ANA 767-300 onto finals to Hong Kong's tricky approach to Runway 13 at Kai Tak International. Twenty seconds later and another flight from Japan's Kansai airport is successfully completed.

offs, for example. The 747, with 17 hull losses by the beginning of 1997 (excluding sabotage and military action), has a rate of just over 1.64 accidents per million departures whereas the DC-10 has a rate of 2.46 and the Airbus A300 a rate of 1.24. These compare to 64 DC-8 hull losses (a rate of 5.61) and 109 hull losses for the 707 and 720 family (just under seven accidents per million departures). New-generation wide-bodies show the increasing trend to improved safety. By early 1997 no Airbus A330s or A340s, Boeing 777s, or McDonnell Douglas MD-11s had been lost while in service.

The revolution in safety is matched by bounding improvements in efficiency. The new aircraft and their engines have more than 30 percent better fuel consumption than the first turbojets. A 777-200, for example, flies almost 100 seat statute miles per U.S. gallon, compared to just over 40 for the 707-320. Successive downturns in the economy and airline business since the start of the 1970s have also forced the industry itself into big improvements in efficiency. This has been particularly

felt in the wide-body arena, where production costs are so huge. As a result, the new generation and its successors have been designed on computers, using advanced lightweight materials to a far greater extent, and are assembled from a larger number of subcontracted parts than ever before. These developments have created other spin-offs. Advanced design and manufacturing processes developed for the 777 were decisive in Boeing's selection as a finalist in the Joint Strike Fighter competition in late 1996. Part of the International Space Station was also created using the same systems.

So where next for the giant jetliner? With passenger growth expected to break the two-billion-per-year mark early in the next century, the role of the wide-body will be increasingly vital in helping the airlines keep pace with demand. Big new super-jumbos currently under study by Airbus will be joined by new, more efficient derivatives of the current wide-body generation. Further off is the promise of more exotic flying wings, blended-wing-body transporters, large supersonic jetliners, and other giant aircraft that have yet to be designed. All will be needed urgently to help keep today's heavily congested air-traffic system from grinding to a complete halt under the coming strain. In that sense, the last three decades have been like a rehearsal for the twenty-first century, when the world is likely to experience the true golden age of the giant jetliner.

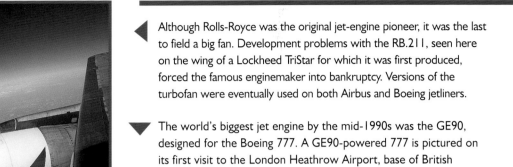

Although Rolls-Royce was the original jet-engine pioneer, it was the last to field a big fan. Development problems with the RB.211, seen here on the wing of a Lockheed TriStar for which it was first produced, forced the famous enginemaker into bankruptcy. Versions of the turbofan were eventually used on both Airbus and Boeing jetliners.

The world's biggest jet engine by the mid-1990s was the GE90, designed for the Boeing 777. A GE90-powered 777 is pictured on its first visit to the London Heathrow Airport, base of British Airways. The huge engine has a 10.25-foot-diameter fan and has produced more than 100,000 pounds of thrust during tests. Note the reflection of a supersonic Concorde on the nacelle.

GENESIS OF THE GIANTS

THE YEAR WAS 1962. The world economy was surging after years in the doldrums following World War II; the Beatles recorded their first hit, "Love Me Do"; basketball's Wilt Chamberlain scored a record 100 points in one game for the Los Angeles Lakers; Richard Burton and Elizabeth Taylor were starring in the outrageously expensive movie *Cleopatra*; Marilyn Monroe died of a drug overdose; and David Lean directed Peter O'Toole in the movie *Lawrence of Arabia*. The United States was frantically trying to catch up with the Soviet Union's surprise lead in space. Telstar, the world's first communications satellite was launched, and John Glenn became the first American to orbit the earth. It was a year to remember.

The biggest global event, however, occurred in October, when the Cold War between the Soviet Union and NATO suddenly threatened to erupt into nuclear conflict. American reconnaissance aircraft flying high over the island of Cuba photographed strange clearings in the tropical forest. These were identified as possible launch sites for intermediate-range nuclear missiles—a suspicion later confirmed when U.S. aircraft snapped shots of missiles en-route to the island aboard Soviet ships. The world held its breath as President John F. Kennedy and Premier Nikita Krushchev faced off. To everyone's relief, the Russians agreed to withdraw the missiles, and the world breathed again.

Project Forecast, Cold War tensions, and the need for an aircraft bigger than the C-141 spawned the giant Lockheed C-5 Galaxy transport and, in doing so, provided the foundations for the first generation of giant jetliners. The diminutive-looking crew gives some clue to the size of this monster as it lumbers along a taxiway at RAF Fairford in the United Kingdom.

General Electric's TF39 was the first big fan engine with the unheard-of bypass ratio of 8:1, or eight times more air passing through the fan compared to the core of the engine. Note the incredible difference in intake size between the GE engine and the B-52's conventional P&W J57 turbojets. The XTF39, as the engine was called for testing, first flew for 1 hour, 45 minutes on June 9, 1967, on this B-52 testbed at Edwards AFB, California. The GE engine, rated at 41,000 pounds of thrust, pumped out the same amount of power as three standard B-52 engines! *General Electric*

Although the Cold War suddenly began to show the first signs of a thaw after the Cuban crisis, the gradual build-up of the Soviet threat over the preceding years had already pushed the U.S. Air Force (USAF) in new directions from which there would be no turning back. The USAF became concerned that its edge over the Soviet Air Force could be lost unless it began looking at its future needs in a more methodical way, rather than simply developing new fighters, bombers, and transports as ad-hoc, one-for-one replacements. So in 1962 it set up Project Forecast, a crystal-ball exercise to review and establish future requirements. The project's leader, Gen. Bernard Schriever, requested data on new technologies from every part of U.S. industry. Some of the information he gathered included intriguing possibilities from General Electric (GE) about new turbofan engines and various fan programs.

The potential for vastly more powerful engines was an appealing prospect to the USAF, which had an aging and largely

State-of-the-art engine technology in the late 1950s was this P&W JT4A. Despite the unusual looking "organ-pipe" exhaust design that mixed the jet exhaust with the passing air, the engine was very noisy and could never be developed to be large enough to power the new giant jetliners.

inadequate strategic airlifter fleet. In the event of a Soviet invasion, the USAF knew it would be hard-pressed to reinforce NATO forces in Europe or anywhere else without modern airlifters. The new high-bypass-ratio engines, as these revolutionary powerplants were called, suddenly created the potential for a giant transporter with huge capabilities. The USAF consequently produced a requirement for a large military airlifter dubbed the CX-HLS (Experimental Cargo/Heavy Logistics System). The performance targets were ambitious, to say the least. The monstrous aircraft was originally required to carry as many as 700 troops, fly 5,500 miles nonstop, and land on unpaved airstrips close to the front line. Such performance was simply not possible with the existing engine technology, so everything depended on the development of the new powerplants.

By 1963 the race was on. To meet the requirement, Pratt & Whitney (P&W) began evaluating turbofan engine designs based on its successful JT3 family and was soon testing hardware. Later that year GE held a competition within its own company to determine the right sort of engine and its exact specifications. A team headed by Don Berkey produced the winning design, which had a huge bypass ratio of 8:1. This meant that eight times more air passed through the fan than through the core of the engine. The fan was made up of a giant set of densely packed blades that churned the air like propellers. An unusual feature was a second set of half-size fan blades arranged behind the first to give what GE loosely called the "stage and a half" design. The second stage enabled GE to reduce the size of the big front fan by around 5 percent, which in turn helped the whole engine to be packaged into a lighter, lower-drag installation.

In March 1964 the USAF told GE to hurry up and get an engine running or it would be out of the competition. In response, GE accelerated plans and laid out a half-scale demonstrator called the GE1/6, which had the 8:1 bypass ratio and a maximum thrust of only 15,830 pounds. This small demonstrator's thrust rating was comparable with the best P&W and Rolls-Royce turbofans then being produced for the Boeing 707, Douglas DC-8, and Vickers VC-10 airliners. With range performance absolutely critical, the demonstrator program, led by Martin Hemsworth, scored big points with the USAF. The engine had a specific fuel consumption (sfc) of less than 0.34 pounds/hour/pound, a drastic reduction over the first jets, which had an sfc of more than 1. Specific fuel consumption is the rate at which fuel is consumed divided by pounds of thrust developed, and thus is, a measure of the engine's efficiency.

With a high level of confidence in its basic idea, GE proposed a full-size engine to the USAF, which had set up a systems program office at Wright Field in Ohio. The company's final written proposal was so huge (90 volumes, with 50 copies of each volume) that it had to be delivered to Wright Field in a tractor-trailer. The effort proved worthwhile, however, because in August 1965 GE was told it had won the competition. Pratt & Whitney's engine bid was penalized for its lack of cooling air in the turbines, a feature that P&W completely revised for the later 747 competition as a result. In September, Lockheed was chosen over Boeing and Douglas to build the big new USAF airframe. General Electric was awarded a contract worth $459,055,600 to develop the new engine, dubbed the TF39. This was the largest single contract GE had ever received.

The production TF39 pumped out an impressive 41,000 pounds of thrust. To get an idea of how big this leap in thrust actually was, the British de Havilland Comet, the first jet airliner to enter service, had made its maiden flight in 1949 with four relatively tiny de Havilland Ghost 50 Mk 1 turbojets. These engines produced 4,450 pounds of thrust each—or roughly the same as some medium-sized biz-jet engines in 1990s terms, but were top performers for their time.

Fifty years later, as the jet airliner enters its fifth decade of development, engine power is already at more than 100,000 pounds of thrust and all because of the wide-body revolution. In other words, the total engine thrust of just one twin-engined Boeing 777 equals the power of more than 11 early Comets!

Engineers expected that the first Comet would need boost power for takeoff, so they built two 5,000-pounds-thrust de Havilland Sprite I rocket motors into the trailing edge between the jet exhausts. This was hardly an acceptable solution in the noise-sensitive environment of later years! As more-powerful engines became available, the Comet grew. The Comet 1A quickly jumped to more-powerful 5,000-pounds-thrust Ghost 50 Mk 2 engines, and by the end of its production life some 15 years later, it was powered by four 10,500-pound-thrust Rolls-Royce Avons.

The Ghost turbojets and Sprite rockets for the Comet were essentially civil versions of military products. This was a consistent theme throughout the 1940s and 1950s when the first Boeing and Douglas commercial jetliners also began life with turbojets based on a military predecessor. In both cases they were powered by the P&W JT3, which was a civil version of the 10,000-pound-thrust J57 turbojet. This powered the F-100 Super Sabre, America's first supersonic fighter, and was used in a slightly altered form on several other aircraft, including the B-52 bomber. The JT3P turbojets powering the prototype 707, or Model 367-80, as it was known, were capable of only 9,500 pounds of thrust.

The world's first successful turbofan to resemble today's designs was the Rolls-Royce Conway, seen here powering an RAF Vickers VC-10 tanker. Rolls called it a bypass turbojet. Although it had only a modest bypass ratio of 0.3:1, it pointed the way to the future.

Turbojets represented a vital step forward, but they often struggled for power on takeoff, particularly in hot air and at high altitude, in which situations they seemed to run out of breath. Airlines wanted more range and payload capability, so the propulsion engineers, in turn, became desperate for more power. Using techniques originally developed during World War II for getting every last horsepower out of the piston engines of the time, they came up with a novel solution that involved pumping water into the combustion chamber. The water would instantly increase the mass going through the engine, effectively fooling the powerplant into believing it was sucking in more air than it really was. The water also temporarily cooled down the raging heat of the turbine area during the critical takeoff period, and although this was less efficient in propulsion terms, it prolonged the life of the hot parts of the engine.

Although takeoff power was dramatically improved, water injection had huge drawbacks and was, at best, a temporary solution. It meant the aircraft had to carry thousands of pounds of dis-

The P&W JT3D turbofan's bypass ratio of 1:1 meant that as much air was expelled by the fan as went through the hot part of the engine. The turbofan transformed the performance of the 707. Although slightly heavier, it increased thrust from around 12,000 pounds to 18,000 pounds, yet had almost exactly the same fuel consumption as the earlier turbojet.

The era of the giant jetliner began with the first flight of the Boeing 747 on a damp February 9, 1969. Note the open blow-in doors around the engine intakes. *Boeing*

tilled water, which took time to load and used up weight that could have been more profitably filled with either passengers, cargo, or more fuel. Secondly, it was an environmental nightmare. Water mixed violently with the products of combustion, ejecting clouds of sooty exhaust that would hang around over the active runway like huge black drapes. Worse still, the bansheelike scream of the turbojet reached new levels of ear-shattering intensity with this method, despite the noise-suppressing "organ pipe" nozzles on each engine.

Far from banning the noisy, dirty jetliners, airports around the world eagerly encouraged jet services by extending runways and expanding terminals. No one wanted to be left behind. Despite the willingness of airports to adapt, the enginemakers knew they had to do better. General Electric and Rolls-Royce both came up with novel methods for increasing power by forcing extra air through the engine. This air was not sucked into the core and burned explosively with fuel, but instead bypassed the gas generator and mixed with the hot exhaust. The result was a cleaner, more efficient powerplant with higher thrust.

In GE's case, the engine was a development of the CJ-805 for the Convair CV-990, a stretched version of the uncompetitive CV-880. The CJ-805-23C, as the engine was called, was made up of a standard -805 turbojet with an "aft fan" section added to the rear. The section was made up of a free-running turbine, cleverly constructed with double-deck blades, the outer portions working on cool intake air in a large diameter "bypass" duct around the engine core (see page 20). The outer blade sections were effectively the distant ancestors of today's big turbofan fan blades and forced air through a double jet nozzle at low velocity. The higher mixing and lower velocity made the engine much quieter than its

Double first: the world's first wide-body jetliner, the Boeing 747, was powered by the first commercial high-bypass-ratio turbofan, the P&W JT9D. At first the marriage was not a happy one, but problems were eventually overcome, and P&W enjoyed a seven-year monopoly on the 747.

15

▲ Although unremarkable compared to the latest generation of big fans, the enormous front fan of the P&W JT9D seemed huge by 1960s standards. Almost 8 feet across, the fan could pump around 1,000 pounds of air per second at full power at sea level. The small ridges inside the intake lip mark the position of blow-in doors that open to allow more air to be sucked into the engine at full power. *Boeing*

predecessors, 40 percent more efficient, and power climbed to a respectable 16,050 pounds of thrust.

The Rolls-Royce Conway, unlike the GE engine, was designed with a large fan at the front of the engine and is credited with being the first true bypass turbofan. The fan was connected to the low-pressure spool of the core and sucked air into both the compressor and the bypass duct. The fan blades not only began the business of compressing the air as it entered the engine core, but performed a dual role as miniature propellers. The engine was used on a special variant of the 707-300, the 707-420, and on the long-range British airliner, the graceful Vickers VC-10.

Not to be left behind, P&W swiftly caught up with Rolls-Royce and GE by developing a turbofan version of its JT3 series. The JT3D-3 turbofan instantly transformed the performance of both the 707 and DC-8 and provided positive proof that turbofans were the civil engine of the future. The emergence of the turbofan also marked the first significant reversal in the historic trend from military to commercial. The idea of a higher-bypass turbofan, originally developed for commercial jetliners, suddenly became useful, if not essential, in a military role—namely, the CX-

HLS. The enginemakers saw that much more advanced high-bypass turbofan technology was the only way to meet the high-thrust and low-fuel-consumption needs of the USAF.

Although GE won the contract for building engines for the CX-HLS, which would eventually reach production as the Lockheed C-5, P&W more than made up for the disappointment by being selected for the Boeing 747 by launch customer Pan Am. General Electric's noisier engine had been a factor against it during the airline's selection process, even in the mid-1960s when the environmental movement was in its infancy. Another reason was price. In January 1966, as GE came up with a more competitive offering, the CF6, rated at 41,100 pounds of thrust, P&W responded by suddenly dropping the engine price from $770,000 per ship set to $690,000. Boeing concluded the P&W-powered version would have a slight edge over the GE-powered version when estimating the operating costs of the big new jetliner. In early comparisons, the P&W version had a direct operating cost of 0.720 cents per statute mile compared with 0.749 for the GE version. This was more than 20 percent cheaper than the operating costs of a smaller 707-321B.

Pratt & Whitney's JT9D was finally selected later that year, signaling the start of a seven-year monopoly on powerplants for the 747 and a crucial head start in the civil "big fan" business. "The advances in the state of the art of aircraft have come with advances in engines, and a lot of airframe people did not like to recognize that," said P&W's Bob Rosati, who was in charge of getting the JT9D engine certified on the 747. Despite being selected as the winner, P&W's problems were only just starting. "We concluded we had a new beast on our hands," said Rosati. "We were pioneering, but didn't know it."

Part of the problem with the early 747 was caused by the growing weight of the aircraft before it even flew. "The aircraft started out at 690,000 pounds [takeoff weight]," Rosati recalled, "so we were planning a 41,000-pound-thrust engine. Then it grew to 710,000 pounds, so we had to get a 42,000-pound engine and then a 43,500-pound engine. It was that final jump that killed us. That last ounce of turbine temperature was the cause of many problems. They were desperate days." To add to the pressure, Boeing had also committed to a rapid build-up in production to meet customer demand and an "aluminum avalanche" was underway in the middle of P&W's problems. "All these aircraft were coming off the line without engines, so they were having to hang cement blocks off them," said Rosati, referring to their temporary solution to the problem encountered by not having the weight of the engines on the wings.

A vital innovation of the big new P&W engine was the use of variable stators, or movable vanes, to carefully control the pressure flow. Again, P&W paid the price for pioneering, as these devices caused problems by jamming. "They worked like a charm and then they'd get stuck solid," said Rosati. "Eventually we found a solution—lots of WD40. I learned to love oil! WD40 saved us, and as an engine man, I'll say we saved the aircraft." The sheer physical size of the new engines led to even more problems. "It was so big and heavy that the engine bowed on takeoff," he continued. "As the aircraft rotated [pitched upward] for takeoff,

Despite its success with the DC-10 tri-jet and A300 twin-jet, GE really wanted to power the 747. After all, what could be better from an enginemaker's point of view than a four-engined jetliner? General Electric engines finally made it onto the aircraft in 1974 when the USAF selected it for the Advanced Airborne Command Post version. A year later the first airline GE 747 was delivered to the Netherlands flag-carrier, KLM.

the wind tried to blow the engine back over the wing. So as the engine bowed, we were rubbing out one side of the compressor shrouds. It began to make a hole in the bottom side of the engine and that really affected stability and performance." The extra weight of the aircraft and the minimal engine power meant the 747 was barely making guarantees as it was, so the new problem was very unwelcome. "You will kill your grandmother for 1 percent better specific fuel consumption!" Rosati remembered saying.

A new engine-support yoke was designed to prevent the "ovalization" of the engine, and P&W later developed a system that cooled the casing. The cooling system gave the blades larger clearances between the tips and casing on takeoff and closed the gap down for the cruise when the engines needed to be running at their most efficient. "You could actually see the fuel flow dropping off as the case cooling came on," Rosati recalled.

Pratt & Whitney was not alone in having problems. The only other major enginemaker for civil wide-bodies, Rolls-Royce, had offered a 44,000-pound-thrust engine called the RB.178 but failed with this and other proposed derivatives to be selected for

either the 747, DC-10, or European Airbus A300 projects. The loss of the Airbus was particularly painful because the British government had negotiated a deal to give design leadership to the French company Sud-Aviation in return for the guaranteed use of the proposed RB.207 engine.

However, fortune smiled on Rolls-Royce when its RB.211 was selected for the Lockheed TriStar project. But trouble was just around the corner, partly because of the unusual configuration of the British engine. Rolls-Royce's design was based on a three-spool arrangement, unlike the GE and P&W engines, which were simpler, two-spool designs. The U.S. engines were made up of a low-pressure and a high-pressure spool, whereas the RB.211 had low-, intermediate-, and high-pressure spools. The British company believed the design would allow each spool to be shorter in length and operate closer to maximum efficiency, thus reducing wear and tear and producing longer life. While the idea was good in principle, it produced a short, stocky engine with a substantial weight penalty. To overcome this and still ensure good performance, Rolls decided to design fan blades from a carbon-fiber material called "Hyfil," which was lighter than conventional titanium. Without the design restrictions of the metal materials, Rolls designed the blades with a wide chord, making them more efficient.

Because the fan was responsible for around 70 percent of the thrust, its development was crucial to the engine's success. It was a bold move to use the new material, and it was years ahead of its time, so Rolls-Royce was venturing into unknown territory.

Increased engine power and greater-than-ever levels of reliability were the foundations for the development of twin-engined giant jetliners such as the A300 and the 767. The vital importance of reliability rose to all-new levels with the start of long over-water flights, commonly called extended-range twin operations, or ETOPS.

Everything looked good to begin with, but problems began cropping up. On one occasion, with the engine mounted on a VC-10 testbed in place of the two left-hand Conways, the blade tips partially disintegrated following a takeoff from a dusty runway and a flight through intense rain.

Tests also revealed serious delamination caused by the different flexing characteristics of the composite and the metal shaft that ran through the core of each blade to stiffen them. With development problems stacking up, Rolls began to go over its fixed-price estimate. The dilemma was made worse by the fact that, despite the British government's assistance with research and development, the inflation rate in the United Kingdom was skyrocketing. Finally, on February 4, 1971, Rolls-Royce declared bankruptcy.

Rolls-Royce was later rescued by the British government, and a new contract was negotiated with Lockheed, which also had

Airbus pioneered the concept of a twin-engined wide-body with the A300. The shorter A310 derivative proved to be a popular medium- and long-range jetliner as well as useful freighter. Note how the engines are pointed, or "toed," inward to balance the force of the thrust on the airframe.

A brand new P&W PW4084 is pictured after being mounted on the wing of an ANA Boeing 777 for the first time at the Boeing facility in Everett, Washington. The fan on the newer engine was 16 inches bigger in diameter than the first generation JT9D and was made up of many fewer wide-chord blades made from hollow titanium.

gone through a massive financial crisis with cost overruns of around $2 billion on the C-5A. The RB.211 was meanwhile fitted with a backup titanium fan and went on to successfully power the TriStar. Rolls-Royce gradually recovered from its bad start and developed bigger and better versions of the RB.211 for the Boeing 747 and 767, as well as a smaller version for the 757. The design also grew into the successful Trent series, which clinched large orders for use on the Airbus A330 and Boeing 777.

Meanwhile, GE began its fight back into the commercial jet-liner business by developing the CF6 family of engines from the basic ingredients of the TF39. The two engines used the same core, but the civil engine had a smaller, 86.5-inch-diameter fan (against 93.5 inches for the military engine) to suit the shorter missions of the wide-bodied airliners. In later years, of course, the CF6 grew in size as mission length grew, and eventually its fan diameter exceeded that of the TF39s. Crucially, GE was also able to develop a quieter fan and small a "quarter-stage" fan immediately behind the main fan rotor.

The delayed breakthrough of GE into the giant civil jetliner arena came in February 1968 when its 40,000-pound-thrust CF6-6 was launched on the first DC-10-10s ordered by American Airlines. The first GE-powered wide-body entered service in 1971 when the DC-10 began airline operations. That same year, Airbus received the first order for the A300 with the GE engine. This was good news for Airbus because many European operators had also

ordered the DC-10 with CF6 engines, and the selection of the same engine for the wide-body twin increased fleet commonality. The Rolls engine was ruled out because the British government withdrew from the Airbus project in 1969, which added to the aforementioned problems of the RB.211 and the lack of government support for a proposed RB.211-61 growth version.

General Electric scored an even bigger success in 1972 when the USAF selected the CF6-50, developed for the A300B, for the Airborne Command Post version of the 747, the E-4A. The Ohio-based engine-maker had been waiting for seven years to get onto the 747, and the company reaped the success of its earlier DC-10 and A300B victories when airlines with these types already in their fleet saw the commonality advantages of GE-powered 747s. These included KLM, Lufthansa, Air France, UTA, ANA, Alia, Air Gabon, Wardair, Pakistan, Thai International, Alitalia, and Philippine Airlines.

Engine development continued to be the pacing factor in wide-body development. The emergence of the big twin jets focused much more attention on reliability than ever before, and this factor attained new levels of urgency in the mid-1980s when twins started flying long-distance over-water flights. These extended-range twin operations (ETOPS) flights lifted expectations of reliability. The GE CF6 series, P&W PW4000 family (which grew out of the JT9D series), and Rolls-Royce RB.211 and later Trent engines were all honed to a much higher level of performance as a result. The trend was easy to read. Most of the attention in the 1970s was focused on lowering fuel consumption, and by the 1980s this shifted to lowering noise. The 1990s began a gradual swing to the vital need for operating consistency.

Dispatch reliability became the key as the airlines found it harder to make money with soaring costs on one side and falling fares and fierce competition on the other. The potential cost of engine failure

Desert sand and debris collects in the intake of an old Convair 990 engine at Mojave, California. The GE CJ805-23 engine was a pioneering "aft-fan" turbofan and could produce up to 16,100 pounds of thrust at full power. At the back of the big duct surrounding the core engine was a set of "bluckets," or blade/buckets made of nickel alloy. The roots of the bluckets were formed into a freely rotating turbine stage, while the upper part was a set of fan blades. Despite its large moment of inertia, the fan lagged the engine power changes by only 0.1 second.

A Cathay Pacific Boeing 777-200 homes in on Boeing Field after a test flight. The aircraft's Rolls-Royce Trent engines were based on the same original three-shaft, or -spool, layout of the RB.211 designed for the TriStar but were capable of more than double the power.

and subsequent delay was increasingly huge with every new jetliner and was simply unacceptable. As the industry moved toward the launch of the proposed giant A3XX and 747-500X/600X jetliners, airline economists began gulping at the prospect of how expensive any delay could be. As a GE executive said, ". . . fuel burn and weight doesn't mean anything compared to dispatch reliability when engine problems make you arrive two hours late at your destination and you have to find room for 600 people in 15 hotels."

Many of the features for the twenty-first century jetliner engine were developed for the Boeing 777, the world's biggest twin-engined aircraft. General Electric started with a clean sheet and produced the world's largest turbofan, the GE90, for the new, big Boeing. With an awesome 10.25-foot-diameter fan, the complete engine was almost the same width as the prototype 707's fuselage! With potential thrust well beyond 115,000 pounds, the GE90 was designed for every present and future version of the 777. Meanwhile, P&W tried a slightly safer approach and produced the PW4084 as a derivative of its PW4000 series. To meet the huge power needs of the 777, the PW4084 was equipped

with a much bigger, 9.3-foot-diameter wide-chord fan. Both engines represented the first commercial application of wide-chord-fan technology for the two U.S. manufacturers. By late October 1996, P&W had started to build the first 98,000-pound-thrust version of the engine for use on the stretched 777-300, which was to become the longest airliner ever to fly. It was expected to fly for the first time around one year later.

The triple-spool philosophy of Rolls-Royce continued with the Trent 800 for the 777. The engine became the first cleared for flight at 90,000 pounds of thrust in January 1995 and was also the

engine that powered the stretched 777-300 on its maiden flight.

When the early 1990s economic slump lifted by 1995, the prospects for a new generation of super-jumbos suddenly appeared to be firmer than ever before. Once again, everything hinged on the availability of the right engines, which could make such monster aircraft economical to operate. The story of these big new powerplants and the super-jumbos is told in Chapter 7. Their development again illustrates how advances in engine technology are intimately linked to the destiny of giant jetliners.

An engine removal during heavy maintenance provides a peep up the inside of the S-duct of a TriStar. The duct did not suffer from the sort of stability problems that had been encountered in earlier jetliners with similar tail-mounted engines because the TriStar's duct was longer.

Airbus's first breakthrough into the vital North American market came when Eastern Airlines signed for 23 A300B4s on April 6, 1978. The whole deal was worth $778 million in hard-money terms but was worth incalculably more to Airbus in terms of global credibility. The A300 "Whisperliner," as the aircraft were dubbed, proved very economical with a measured fuel-per-seat-mile on the airline's routes 20 percent lower than for the TriStars and 34.6 percent lower than for the 727s.

2
CONCEPTS AND HURDLES

ASK ANYONE WHICH IS THE MOST RECOGNIZABLE WIDE-BODY and he or she will probably name the Boeing 747. With its distinctive upper-deck hump, the "Jumbo Jet" remains one of the most memorable jetliners built. The McDonnell Douglas DC-10 and MD-11 and Lockheed L-1011 TriStar, each distinguished by an engine in the tail, are also easily picked out at any airport. However, from the Airbus A300 onward, the modern generation of western wide-body twins—the A310, A330, Boeing 767, and even the much-larger 777—all look very similar to the untutored eye. Only the four-engined A340 and Russian-made Ilyushin Il-86 and -96 break the twin-jet mold.

Why, then, is there such a wide variety of shapes and sizes, and what made the designs of these early wide-bodied jetliners so different from the later generations? By definition, all of them share a wide fuselage designed to carry many passengers, so what factors influenced their final configuration, and what design hurdles were overcome to create them?

The story begins with the 747. This was the first wide-body jetliner ever launched and deserves the credit for starting the era of the giant jetliner. In many ways, its final shape was heavily influenced by competition from another kind of aircraft. When it was under design in the mid-1960s, everyone believed that supersonic aircraft would soon dominate the world of air travel. The 747 was being pushed mainly by Pan American, which wanted a low-cost people-mover. The airline needed a big aircraft quickly to keep capacity in line with demand, particularly on trunk routes such as New York to London and Paris. The airline knew that the big three U.S. airframe makers were all chasing the CX-HLS competition and that the technology required for a much bigger commercial airliner was becoming available.

It took the once-mighty Pan Am and its visionary president Juan Trippe to launch the 747 into reality with an order for 25 of the aircraft in April 1966. *Clipper Ocean Spray*, the twenty-fifth 747 built, is pictured here taxiing for takeoff ahead of another fleet member in June 1989. Later in life, this 747 was bought by GE and used as a flying testbed for new engines, including the GE90.

But even Pan Am was convinced that the long-term future lay with faster, rather than bigger, aircraft. It had even put its name down for a fleet of supersonic Concorde airliners then in development by the United Kingdom's British Aircraft Corporation and Sud Aviation of France. Even as Pan Am was discussing the embryonic 747 with Boeing, it was one of 18 airlines that had placed commitments for up to 80 Concordes.

Boeing was the first to see the 747 in the same light, as recalled by former chief 747 engineer Joe Sutter, "The thing that affected the design of the 747 was the fact that there was this SST [supersonic transport] lurking in the background, and people felt that the airplane might end up being a cargo airplane. So from the start we designed it as a cargo airplane."

From its earlier studies, Boeing knew that all the airlines were in favor of putting up to 350 passengers into its new airplane. So, having decided that the 747 would also be a good cargo aircraft, Boeing now had to work out what sort of size to make the main deck. Pan Am, among others, had argued that a double-decker would be a good design. Why not simply put a stretched 707 fuselage on top of another and, hey, presto! create a 350-

The 747 could have looked very different from the final design that survived into production. Three finalists were double-deck designs of varying capacity, at least one of which was fitted with a wing located midway up through the fuselage. One design, bottom left, was nicknamed the anteater because of the low, drooping flight-deck position. The eventual winner, differentiated from the similar design at bottom right by the outboard engine locations, is at bottom center. *Boeing*

The unprecedented cross-sectional volume of the 747 is evident in this slice of a forward fuselage section once used for fatigue research. By widening the main cabin to 20 feet and fairing the flight deck into the top of the fuselage, Boeing effectively created a triple decker. Cargo normally fills the hold, though people are sometimes accommodated in some military and VIP versions.

seater? The idea seemed appealing until Boeing began to look closely at the details.

Sutter, who became known in the industry as the "father of the 747," takes up the story: "Everybody was intrigued with double-deckers. Some of the preliminary designs were double-deckers but the group working for me decided that was the wrong way to go, and right near the contract-signing date we conceived this wide single-deck design." So what made Boeing change its mind? "If you have, say, a 500- or 600-passenger airplane," Sutter continued, "you have a big wing on a short, stubby airplane and the servicing of the aircraft, the door arrangement, the emergency evacuation situation and the loading of cargo and baggage all becomes a problem. It's just a clumsy airplane. If you have a short airplane and you put 550 or 600 passengers in it, there's no room for any cargo and hardly enough room for the passengers' baggage. On top of that, putting systems in the aircraft is hard. It just does not work."

Having decided against a double-decker and opting for a single deck, Boeing then faced another critical decision. How wide should it be? In the end cargo was the deciding factor in the

width decision, the most crucial ever made by the designer of any jetliner. "Supposing the airplane does a few years in service over the North Atlantic and, say around 1975, they replace it with a twice-daily-return Concorde service and rip out the seats, what makes the most sense from the cargo point of view?" asked the engineers. They already knew that up to 350 people would have to sit on the single deck, so the area would be wide. The designers placed two 8 x 8=foot seagoing containers on the deck and sketched a circle around them. The resulting cabin cross-section was around 20 feet in diameter (19 feet, 5 inches in initial drawings, later to grow to 20 feet, 2 inches with changes to the inside trim) and would seat 10 or even 11 abreast in economy class, providing room for up to 400.

One more major decision was taken to create the familiar 747 shape that we know so well today. If the airplane was to be a freighter, it should, they argued, have straight-in nose-loading/unloading capability. The nose would be able to tilt up like a movable visor, providing instant access to the voluminous interior. The flight deck could not realistically hinge on the nose section, particularly if it was to hinge upward rather than sideward, as on other front-loader cargo airplanes. It was therefore decided to move the cockpit up and out of the way onto an upper-deck level. At first, the design had the cockpit scabbed onto the fuselage like a blister, similar to the Douglas Globemaster of an earlier generation or the Vickers Viscount, a British turboprop airliner. This was a practical solution from an engineering perspective, as it made the fuselage simpler to make and pressurize. Unfortunately, the wind tunnel studies proved otherwise and revealed the blister as a big drag generator at the high speeds Boeing was contemplating.

Boeing therefore faired the flight deck more gradually into the upper fuselage, creating a gently curved hump. The cockpit structure was more prominent as a result and produced an unusual slab-sided cross-section. As circles are much more aerodynamic and easier to pressurize than flat-sided shapes, the front of the 747 required strengthening to cope with the higher structural loads. The upper deck and the fairing behind it was originally intended for crew only. When Pan Am president Juan Trippe visited Seattle to view progress on the first 747, he noticed the apparently unused area behind the cockpit. On hearing the area was earmarked as a probable crew rest area, Trippe insisted that it should be converted into a lounge for his first-class passengers. Eventually a circular stairway was developed to connect the upper deck with the main deck, and the double-decker was reborn, on a limited scale, at least. The upper deck was stretched in the later life of the 747, growing in seating capacity from eight in the first 747-100s to 16 in the first -200s and up to 32 in 747s built after 1974. The upper deck was stretched even further on the later 747-300s and -400s, providing room for up to 69 in normal configurations, and the proposed development of the 747-500X and -600X would have pushed this up to nearly 100. Not bad for an area that started life as space for a couple of crew rest bunks and seats!

Another characteristic feature of the 747 is the aircraft's sharply swept wing. It might have been even more sharply

▲ Aircraft number four flies high over eastern Washington during the test program. This aircraft was eventually delivered to Pan Am as *Clipper Bostonian* in July 1970 and was ultimately converted into a freighter for Evergreen International Airlines in 1993. *Boeing*

▼ The reason for the 747's characteristic hump is captured in this picture of an Evergreen 747 freighter ready to load up for another flight at John F. Kennedy International, New York. Boeing believed most 747s would eventually be converted into cargo aircraft, in addition to a large number built on the line as freighters. Boeing therefore, designed the nose to hinge upward to enable cargo to be loaded straight onto the main deck, and the cockpit had to be moved up and out of the way. This particular 747 was the 237th built, and it first flew in May 1974.

swept—to around 40 degrees—if Pan Am had its way, but the manufacturer finally settled on a slightly less dramatic 37.5 degrees. In the mid-1960s, state-of-the-art wing design decreed that the only way to make an aircraft cruise faster on the same power was to make the wing thinner or sweep it back sharply. Boeing managed to achieve a bit of both without incurring the classic problems usually associated with these design features. Thinner wings normally need thicker, and hence heavier, skins for extra compensatory strength. In the case of the 747, which had two engines mounted on each wing, the bending relief moment of the heavy engines helped hold down the wing against its natural tendency to lift. The result was a flexible wing that did not require vast amounts of internal strengthening. Sharply swept wings usually make for poor low-speed handling and for high take-off and landing speeds, hence a requirement for longer runways. Boeing cleverly packed the wing with sophisticated flaps and slats that allowed the 747 to fly slowly and use the same runways as the 707.

The big jetliner would not be able to land on the same runways as other aircraft if it cracked the concrete or asphalt every time. To spread the runway-crushing weight of the 300-ton monster, Boeing designed it with double the normal number of under-

▶ The sheer leap in scale represented by the 747 often had to be seen to be believed. The 747 had more than double the capacity of the 707, seen peeping into view on the right hand side of this aerial view of jetliners in storage at Marana, Arizona. Note the tiny Fokker F28 twinjets, one of which is tucked in below the 747's horizontal stabilizer.

▲ Despite the huge size of the 747, Boeing designed it to use the same runways as much smaller jetliners of the day. To help slow the aircraft for landing and to shorten take-off runs, the wing was fitted with huge triple-slotted flaps. The first slot is between the trailing edge of the wing and the first section of flap.

carriage legs. Two main four-wheel bogies or trucks were located in the standard wing-root position, but an additional two bogies, again each with four wheels, were placed slightly aft, directly beneath the belly. By doubling the number of main undercarriage wheels, Boeing was able to use 707-size tires and wheels, keeping the advantage of commonality.

Trijets

The development of the big-fan engines and the 747 created a host of new possibilities for airlines and, ironically, manufacturers other than Boeing. American Airlines recognized the potential for a new large-capacity domestic transport that would use engines similar to those used on the 747.

In April 1966, the airline issued a requirement for an aircraft with the same range and landing/takeoff performance as the 727 but with roughly double the passenger capacity. It wanted an aircraft that could carry a full load of passengers plus 5,000 pounds of freight from Chicago to Los Angeles at Mach 0.8. It asked manufacturers for the capability to fly 1,850 nautical miles from a 9,000-foot runway, at a takeoff temperature of 90 degrees Fahrenheit. For shorter-range routes, say New York to Chicago,

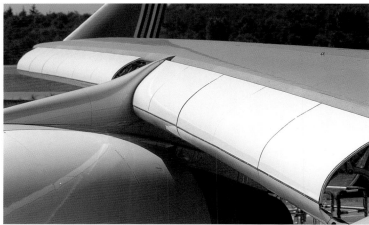

▲ The leading, or front, edge of the 747 wing was also fitted with Krueger flaps, which can be varied in curvature, or camber, to increase lift at low speeds. Rigid Kruegers equip the inboard leading edge.

the same aircraft would have to be able to take off at the same high temperatures with a full payload from much smaller runways, such as those at La Guardia Airport.

Douglas Aircraft and Lockheed, big names in the U.S. airliner business, had both been toying with "jumbo" jet designs and eagerly tackled the specifications with twin-engined designs seating more than 300. As more U.S. domestic airlines saw the plans, it became obvious that a slightly longer-range aircraft capable of distances from Los Angeles to New York, would be more popular. Quite independently, both aircraftmakers went back to the drawing board and came back with three-engined designs that would not only be able to fly further but could still make money flying short distances. The trijet idea also held other advantages in these early days of big-fan development when power and reliability were still questionable. A three-engined jet would be able to fly longer over-water routes, would have greater weather limits for takeoff and landing, could be ferried back to a maintenance base with one engine inoperative, and would be more efficient at take-off in hot weather and at high altitude.

Douglas and Lockheed still kept their big-twin concepts alive until late 1967 when the biggest U.S. domestic airlines really started to warm to the idea of a 300-seat tri-jet. After some stiff market competition with "paper" designs stretching and shrinking to meet as many needs as possible, Lockheed launched its L-1011 TriStar in March 1968 with large orders for 144 from TWA, Eastern, and a U.K.-based financial group called Air Holdings. The latter held sales rights to all territories outside the United States, and initial purchases were underwritten by London bankers to give Lockheed a bridgehead into the export market. The deal would also offset the purchase of the Rolls-Royce RB.211 engines with which Lockheed had chosen to power the TriStar, its first commercial airliner since the Electra turboprop.

Douglas, by now backed financially by McDonnell, actually won the first tri-jet order on February 19, 1968, when it was selected by American Airlines to supply 25 of the aircraft. But even though this included options for another 25, McDonnell Douglas did not think this was enough of an order to justify the full go-ahead of the DC-10 TriStar, as the new tri-jet was named, due to its logical ordering sequence behind the DC-8 and DC-9. With the go-ahead of the TriStar given the next month, things began looking a bit bleak for the DC-10. Then, on April 25, United Air Lines ordered 30 DC-10s, with options on another 30, and the program was launched.

Because both new tri-jets were designed around roughly the same passenger capacity and freight volume, the two were virtually identical. The DC-10 ended up with a 20-foot diameter and an 18-foot, 9-inch-wide cabin, while Lockheed's TriStar fuselage was 2 inches wider internally because of the position of the floor. The Lockheed design, like the DC-10's, was the end result of countless trade studies. Lockheed's original idea was a nine- or 10-abreast layout, but it found that on an 1,800-mile range this would create a weight penalty of 7,000 pounds relative to an eight-abreast layout with two aisles. Although it stuck with the same layout, it increased the final cross-section from 224 inches to 235 inches to provide more internal room. McDonnell Douglas was partially influenced by the 747 design, and all but the forward pair of main-deck entry doors were designed to be 42-inches wide to give jetway compatibility with the big Boeing.

Similarities existed between both wing designs. Both makers decided it was not worth trying to equal the 747's design speed of Mach 0.88, so they aimed instead for cruise Mach numbers close to 0.85. Both ended up with a sweep angle of 35 degrees measured at the usual point a quarter of the way back through the width (or chord) of the wing. Lockheed worked out that a flight time within 15 minutes of the 747's would be competitive on transcontinental flights. It also estimated that attempting to push up speed to Mach

The 300-plus-ton weight of the fully loaded 747 had to be spread to prevent it cracking the runway on landing or to stop it from simply sinking through the tarmac on the apron. By dividing up the main landing gear into four legs, Boeing was also able to use 707-size tires, saving on costs and improving commonality.

0.88 would have needed 30,000 pounds extra takeoff weight and 16 percent bigger engines, besides adding to the direct operating cost by more than seven precious percentage points.

Although both new tri-jets were remarkably similar, one feature made them as different as chalk and cheese. The two companies had adopted radically different solutions to the best position of the tail-mounted engine. The DC-10 engine was mounted in the tail fin itself and hung on a strut that was cantilevered aft of the fin spar. The inlet was supported by a large banjo-shaped fitting that allowed air to enter the jet head-on. The TriStar, on the other hand, enclosed the tail engine right at the back of the fuselage at the base of the fin. Air was ducted into the engine through a huge S-shaped intake, or S-duct.

McDonnell Douglas believed its tail location was superior to Lockheed's because the performance of the DC-10 center engine would be almost identical to the other two wing-mounted engines. In other tail-mounted designs with S-duct inlets such as the 727 or

Evening sunlight picks out the elegant curves of the "S-duct" that feeds air to the TriStar's tail, or number-two, engine. At first, the airlines were skeptical about Lockheed's claims that the serpentinelike intake would not affect the performance of the engine.

Hawker Siddeley Trident, the tail engine needed special thrust-settings to match it to the other engines. The flow of air entering the serpentine duct was sometimes distorted, making the engine sensitive to cross-wind takeoffs and causing slower acceleration. The simpler tail-high installation freed it from nearly all of these restrictions and gave it common settings, compatibility with the systems on the other engines, and a common installation. It could also be removed easily by swinging down the tail cone and the two inner halves of the elevators.

The unusual tail structure presented some interesting challenges to McDonnell Douglas, as recalled by former Douglas engineering vice president Dale Warren: "We looked at five different design concepts including an S-duct," he said. "In the end, we ended up with a straight-through duct, which required the use of enormous forgings to span the duct. These forgings weighed around 5,000 pounds, and when they came out of the workshop they weighed about 500 pounds by the end. They were the largest forgings in the world at the time, and we patented them."

The structure of the wing-fuselage join area was also cleverly designed to avoid transferring excess bending moments between the fuselage and the wing, and vice-versa. "When the wing flexed it usually made the fuselage egg shaped," continued Warren, "so we decided that if we could reconfigure that fuselage ovalization, it could help trap some energy. We therefore cantilevered the bulkhead to form a trapezoidal structure so the effective wheelbase was larger." The company also stiffened up the engine-mounting pylons on the wings by adding around 500 pounds to each to offset any potential flutter effects.

Meanwhile, Lockheed chose its tail location after an intensive trade study whittled the final configuration down to four different solutions, including a straight-through DC-10-style intake. The S-duct was longer and less kinked than the 727 or Trident, so Lockheed said the inlet performance was hardly different from a standard inlet. Wind-tunnel tests proved the intake would be efficient in cross winds up to 50 knots. The design was further defended by engineers saying the drag was lower around this type of tail, and the layout allowed more of the aft cabin to be used for floor area. The lower engine position also allowed Lockheed to design the TriStar with a bigger rudder. Together with a lower center of gravity, due to the lower engine position, the large rudder meant directional control was good. This, in turn, allowed Lockheed to place the wing-mounted engines farther outboard than those on the DC-10. On both aircraft the jets were slung out forward of the wings on pylons. This position used the weight of the engine to counteract the tendency of the wing to twist and lift, allowing Lockheed to design a lighter wing structure.

"The centerline position was really adopted for two main reasons: thrust pattern and convenience of maintenance," said Lockheed TriStar chief engineer Elliott Green. "With this position, the engine could be attended to with a platform 20 feet off the ground; on the DC-10 it was another 10 feet or so higher, so they had to put a maintenance platform in the cowling that folded down." Despite the logic of the location, Lockheed found a lot of resistance to the idea. "There was considerable doubt on the part of the airlines because of the S-duct," continued Green. "But we did our homework on that and we had a much less tight S than on the 727, so our S-duct worked out very nicely."

The distinctive flap-track fairings of the A300B wing are prominent in this twilight view. The "roof-top," or aft-loaded cross section design of the Airbus wing was one of the consortium's many technical firsts. Others include an automatic device to push power to maximum in case of wind shear and the double use of generators on each engine to produce power for a third set of back-up systems.

Airbus

The year 1965 was just as a pivotal for aerospace in Europe as it was in the United States. At that year's Paris air show, informal meetings took place between several major European airlines, including Air France, Alitalia, BEA (forerunner to British Airways), Lufthansa, Sabena, and SAS. All were trying to sketch out their requirements for a new short-to-medium-haul airliner to meet the higher passenger loads then being forecast for the 1970s. The European Airbus, although still far off at that stage, can trace its roots to this meeting, which started a chain reaction among aircraft and enginemakers, as well as European governments.

At the end of 1965, Hawker Siddeley began working with French counterparts Breguet and Nord in response to an airline airbus specification produced by an Anglo-French government working party. The group produced several designs, including the HBN100, a twin-engined, low-wing jetliner capable of carrying 225 with a potential stretch capacity of more than 260. The HBN100 was chosen for further study, and the consortium was

The low-mounted, centerline thrust of the tail engine allowed Lockheed to place the other engines farther out on the wing than those on the DC-10. The Lockheed design therefore obtained more bending relief from the weight of the wing engines. Here a TriStar belonging to now-defunct launch customer Eastern taxies at Miami.

Some operators, such as Delta, upgraded their TriStar 1 aircraft to improve range and performance well after Lockheed stopped making the big jetliner. This aircraft was converted into an L-1011-250 in 1987. It was fitted with more-powerful 50,000-pound-thrust RB.211 engines and maximum takeoff weight was raised to 510,000 pounds, almost 20 percent more than the original version. This gave it the "legs" to fly long-range routes such as London to the U.S. West Coast, and at last allowed it to compete head-on with its arch rival, the DC-10-30.

The first DC-10 cruises high over California on its maiden flight on August 29, 1970, when chief project pilot Clifford Stout flew the aircraft from Long Beach to Edwards AFB. The flight lasted 3 hours and 26 minutes and included a top speed of 345 miles per hour at a maximum altitude of more than 30,000 feet. *McDonnell Douglas*

joined by Sud Aviation of France and Arbeitsgemeinschaft Airbus, which represented German manufacturers. The new group formed the nucleus of what was eventually to become Airbus Industrie, a Groupement d'Interet Economique set up in December 1970.

The project, now named the A300, made slow but gradual progress through the mire of governmental red tape and international negotiations. In 1967, the British, French, and German governments signed a memorandum of understanding to go ahead with the first phase of developing the aircraft. Various changes resulted in the aircraft being scaled down from a 300- to 250-seater and renamed the A300B, and airline interest appeared to be wavering on the basis that the Airbus was growing "too big." The British government bailed out in April 1969. Germany and France agreed to carry on without the British government, though the United Kingdom's Hawker Siddeley maintained its links as the wing supplier.

By May 1969 when the A300B was formally launched, the fuselage diameter was fixed at 18 feet, 6 inches to provide room for eight seats across with twin aisles. Airbus officials regarded the term "wide-body" as rather vulgar, so they preferred to refer to the new design as a "twin-aisle." The company had earlier rejected a 19-foot, 6-inch fuselage because, among other things, it was felt that many operators would not be able to resist fitting an extra seat in the addi-

▼ American Airlines got value for money from its DC-10 fleet which it ordered, as launch customer, on February 19, 1968. Toward the end of its career with American some of the DC-10 fleet was bartered to Federal Express in exchange for hush kits. Federal Express turned the aircraft into freighters while American "hushed" some of its surviving Boeing 727-200s.

tional 12 inches instead of providing bigger seats or more space, giving the Airbus the reputation of being overcrowded. The cross-section was also perfectly circular, like the fuselages of the DC-10 and L-1011, and had been fortuitously enlarged by four inches at the last minute to enclose two under-floor LD3 freight containers, which were just starting to become the new standard.

Even as the A300B1 flew for the first time on October 28, 1972, the aircraft had already started to grow again in response to demands from the sole firm customer, Air France. Only two B1s were built. They were immediately followed by the A300B2, which became the standard-production version. The B2 was lengthened 8 feet, 7 inches by the insertion of five fuselage frames, and it could carry an additional 24 seats, taking total capacity to 301 in a typical all-economy layout. The company also quickly developed a B4 version, doubling the range to more than 3,000 nautical miles with a typical load of around 250 passengers and bags.

The wing design was among the major innovations. The wing was originally developed by aerodynamicists at Hawker Siddeley's (formerly de Havilland's) Hatfield design center and was much deeper, or thicker, than comparable wings. It made use of what was known as the "aft-loaded" principle, which develops lift over most of the upper surface of the wing instead of confining it to a relatively thin strip just behind the leading edge, as do most conventional jetliner wings.

Looking side on, it almost looked as if the wing had been attached to the fuselage upside down. Instead of the classic wing cross-section with a curved upper surface and flat lower surface, the new wing looked exactly the opposite. Instead of a sharp leading edge, it was relatively blunt. The top surface was flatter, and the

A grand total of 446 DC-10s were built, 60 of which were KC-10 tanker versions for the USAF. By 1979, when this picture was taken of the busy predelivery ramp at Douglas Aircraft's Long Beach, California, site, the line was increasingly dominated by the DC-10-30. Although DC-10-30 production lasted 18 years, half of the total civil versions were delivered in the first four years, and 85 percent of deliveries had been completed by the end of 1980. The slight increase in -30 wingspan compared to the -10 is visible by comparing the wing tips of the two aircraft at bottom right. The Garuda aircraft is a -30. *McDonnell Douglas*

underside bulged down. The effect was so dramatic that virtually every large commercial jetliner has since followed suit. The new wing worked better because, as air hit the blunt leading edge, it would still accelerate but not as rapidly as over a sharp-edged conventional wing. As a result, the air sped up more gradually as it passed back over the wing. In more conventional wings, such as the 707, the air dramatically accelerated to the point that it reached supersonic speeds before the rest of the aircraft was anywhere near the speed of sound. The air then formed a shock wave over the wing, which caused drag.

The advantages of the new wing, which was also called a "rooftop" section, were tremendous. Although the supersonic

Some airlines, including Northwest, needed longer range and higher payload capability. In response, Douglas developed the heavier DC-10-30 and -40 series. It featured a wider, 165-foot, 4-inch wingspan, more-powerful engines, and a center gear leg to support the heavier weight of fuel carried in the belly between the wings. The GE-powered -30 series was the best selling version of the DC-10 with 266 being built. The P&W-powered -40, like this Northwest example, sold less well with only 42 being built.

shock wave still occurred at high cruise speeds, its onset was delayed, so the aircraft could fly up to Mach 0.85, compared to Mach 0.81 or 0.82 in a similarly powered conventional-winged aircraft. Engineers could also make the thicker wing with thinner aluminum skin, saving weight. The wing could achieve higher speeds without needing to be swept back at such sharp angles, giving the jetliner better handling at slower speeds. Finally, the deep wing could hold huge volumes of fuel, a factor that would come into play later in the life of the Airbus family when the same basic structure provided the capacity for up to one-third more fuel without major redesign.

Airbus also notched up a few more technological firsts with the A300, including an auto-throttle system that controlled the engines throughout the entire flight. It was also the first big jetliner with only two engines to have triple-redundant power and control systems. In addition, the A300 also had the first system to automatically react against a phenomenon called "wind shear." This is a condition in which the wind suddenly, and often violently, changes direction and strength. If this occurs when the aircraft is coming in to land with its engines at a low power setting, the results could be

continued on page 38

The prototype A300 takes shape in Toulouse in 1972. Only two A300B1s were built, as the first production aircraft were slightly longer A300B2. This aircraft made a successful first flight on October 28, 1972, becoming the world's first wide-body twin jet. Sadly, this historic aircraft was later broken up, though some parts were preserved at Le Bourget, Paris. *Airbus Industrie*

FOLLOWING

A Gulf Air TriStar approaches London Heathrow on a rare clear January day in 1991. At this time of year, the crew was normally using the aircraft's full-blind landing system. The TriStar was the first wide-body to be certified with such a system, and within months of entering service, aircraft used by Eastern and Delta were, on several occasions, the only jetliners able to operate in bad weather.

Air France launched the very first A300B2 into service in 1974 when it flew from Paris to London on May 23 carrying 25 first-class and 225 coach-, or economy-class, passengers. More than 20 years later the airline still operated the first aircraft, F-BVGA, which was originally delivered to it on May 10, 1974.

The DC-10 tail engine inlet is slightly oval with the inlet lips thickened on the side. This was designed to keep the flow of air into the inlet smooth even at the most severe condition, a high crosswind.

Much of the 14,000 hours of wind tunnel testing Douglas conducted on the DC-10 design was concentrated on the unusual tail configuration. Tests revealed that the straight inlet duct produced very little drag, and of that, most was due to skin friction rather than the shape of the tail unit itself. The polished tail cone, seen here on this Aero Peru DC-10, can be hinged down to allow the engine to be lowered for removal. The inboard part of each elevator also drops down to provide space for the engine. The split line is clearly visible at the bottom of the picture.

Continued from page 35

disastrous. The aircraft could be literally pushed down into the ground or simply lose flying speed, stall, and crash. The Airbus system detected the condition and immediately adjusted power to help the crew steer out of trouble. In later years this reactive system was replaced in most giant jetliners with a predictive system that looked ahead and anticipated the problem, rather than reacting to it once it had begun.

In addition to being technologically advanced, the A300 was also the world's largest twin-engined wide-body when it made its first flight on October 28, 1972. The first production A300B2 flew in April 1974 and entered service with Air France the following month. The international battle of the wide-bodies had finally begun.

▲ Airbus soon penetrated new markets beyond Europe and the United States. Its wide-body twins were soon in service in every major region, including Latin America, where, by early 1997, the Airbus A300/A310 family had clinched more than half the market for 200–250-seat aircraft. One early operator was VIASA of Venezuela which leased this 1979-built A300B4 in the late 1980s.

▼ Iberia-owned *Doana*, the 130th A300B built, demonstrates spritely takeoff performance thanks to powerful engines and high-lift devices which are clearly illuminated in this late afternoon departure from Bristol in the United Kingdom. The Fowler flaps on the trailing edge of the wing cover 84 percent of each semi-span and increase the chord of the wing by 25 percent when fully extended. Early flight tests showed that the high-lift system was so much better than predicted that two flap settings were deleted for takeoff.

Western avionics and engines were used for the first time in the Il-96M. A suite of Rockwell Collins digital avionics gave the Russian jetliner's cockpit a distinctly Western feel. The display was dominated by six CRT displays which showed navigation, primary flight, engine, and systems status in the usual way. Only the cyrillic characters of the Russian alphabet (named after the ninth century monk, St. Cyril) used on the panel and several controls give away the aircraft's true origins.

It is rumored that Richard Branson, the owner of Virgin Atlantic, negotiated a better deal for his A340s by betting the Airbus president, Jean Pierson, that he could remove the Frenchman's wristwatch without him knowing. Branson then apparently hypnotized Pierson and successfully removed his watch. The exact discount is unknown!

GROWING, SHRINKING, AND STRETCHING

Snow lay thick on the ground at the old Moscow Central Airport of Khodinka as A. Kuznetsov, Hero of the Soviet Union, lined up the prototype Ilyushin Il-86 for its maiden flight on a cold December day in 1976. The four NK-86 turbofans spooled up to their maximum 28,660 pounds of thrust, sucking in the frigid air and whirling snow from all directions. The Il-86 bucked and swayed until Kuznetsov released the brakes. The runway at the Ilyushin Design Bureau's base was short, only 5,970 feet long, and the big jetliner seemed to be gathering speed too slowly to make it. After a few agonizing seconds, which seemed more like minutes to anxious onlookers, Kuznetsov and his copilot hauled back on the control column and the Il-86 roared into the sky with just 400 feet of runway to spare! The Soviet Union had joined the growing wide-body clan.

Like the rest of the world, the Soviet Union saw rapid growth in demand for passenger and freight capacity. In the late 1960s Aeroflot, the U.S.S.R. national carrier, issued a requirement for an "airbus" to the three main civil design bureaus—Antonov, Tupolev, and Ilyushin. Ilyushin won the competition with a wide-body design loosely based on its Il-62 long-range transport. This configuration had "borrowed" from the British VC-10 design, which had four jets clustered together at the rear of the aircraft beneath a tall T-tail. Even the Russians later openly admitted the rather blatant copying of the design, saying imitation was the sincerest form of flattery!

One of Aeroflot Russian International Airlines Il-86 fleet with the revised gray tail color scheme, pictured at Moscow's Sheremetyevo airport. Note the "fences" on the upper surface of the wing which are aligned with the engines to improve aerodynamic performance by countering the outward, or spanwise, airflow.

The first wide-body ever made in the former Soviet Union, the Il-86 registered CCCP-86000, now resides at the Institute of Civil Engineering at Kiev-Zhulyani, Ukraine. The weather-beaten aircraft first flew in December 1976 and still carries the display number "348" painted on it for its attendance at the 1979 Paris Air Show. Including this aircraft, a total of 103 commercial Il-86s were made.

The much larger size of the new aircraft and the lack of bending relief of the uncluttered wing meant the embryonic Ilyushin wide-body would hardly have enough power to take off. It was years away from the possibility of operating profitably as an airliner. The design therefore changed to the inevitable wing-mounted engine layout. Like the DC-10's and L-1011's, the Il-86's wing was swept back to 35 degrees and, like the 747's and A300's, it incorporated a third spar in the inner wing to give it extra strength in case of a catastrophic engine failure and breakup.

Unlike the U.S. and Airbus aircraft, which were designed to operate between sophisticated domestic and international airports, the Il-86 was meant to be a rugged mass transport primarily for the long intra-U.S.S.R. routes. Airports in far-off Tashkent and Siberia were not equipped with air-bridges and jetways, and in comparison with most Western equivalents, were very basic. Ilyushin therefore designed a practical, very Russian solution. The big jet would have three air-stair doors on the lower deck through which up to 350 passengers entered the port side. One door would be ahead of the wing, the others behind. The passengers would then stow their hand baggage and thick winter coats in the lower deck "closet" before climbing one of three fixed stairs to the main deck.

Instead of using the big, rugged air-stair doors, made in the industrial town of Kharkov, Aeroflot had the option of using four main-deck doors at airports with jetways. The inner stairs could also be deleted in one version, saving more than 6,600 pounds and freeing up space for 25 more seats. Another first for a Russian-built airliner was a central main undercarriage leg, similar in most respects to the design of the main landing gear on the heavier -30 and -40 versions of the DC-10.

The Il-86 was a quantum leap in size over any other commercial jet that flew in the Soviet Union when it was introduced into service in 1980. Many of the airfields were simply not equipped with air bridges or stairs tall enough to reach the main deck level, so the Ilyushin was fitted with three air-stair doors in the lower deck of the port side. Passengers climb up the stairway fitted to the inside of the hinged door, place coats and hand baggage in lockers on the lower deck, and climb up the stairs to the right of the picture to the main deck.

This Il-86, operated by Kazair, clearly shows the position of the three hinged air-stair doors as it sits on the ramp of Moscow's Domodedovo airport awaiting the return flight to Alma-Ata. Kazair was the newly established national airline of Kazakhstan, one of the most fortunate of the independent states of the Russian Federation. With a population of around 17 million, the country kept the airline busy transporting goods and people to and from the its vast reaches which embrace a million square miles of steppe, desert, and mountains. Trade is expected to increase as Kazakhstan is rich in natural resources, including fertile farmland in the northern plateau, and huge oil reserves.

Despite the main innovations, the range performance of the Il-86 was generally disappointing. On flights from Moscow to Havana, Cuba, for example, the aircraft had to be refueled at Shannon on the west coast of Ireland and in Gander, on the east coast of Canada. In response to the problems, Ilyushin undertook a major redesign of the aircraft. The result was the Il-96-300.

The new aircraft was shrunk by 13 feet, 9 inches, trading airframe weight for range capability. In addition, it was given a new wing with a "super-critical" or aft-loaded cross-section, reduced sweep, and greater span with winglets. New "Westernized" avionics were introduced, as was a fly-by-wire flight-control system. It also had more powerful 35,275-pound-thrust engines developed by the Soloviev Design Bureau. These PS-90 turbofans had a much higher bypass ratio than the NK-86s and were similar to the second-generation P&W PW2000 and Rolls-Royce RB.211-

The first Il-96-300 makes a steep turn during a display at the 1989 Paris air show. The aircraft was the first of five prototypes and had flown at Khodinka for the first time less than a year before. Although externally similar to the Il-86, the 96-300 was fitted with new structural materials and technology to extend its life to at least 60,000 hours and 12,000 landings. Note the winglets at the tips of the new supercritical wings. The big jetliner was the first Russian commercial transport with fly-by-wire controls.

One of the main reasons for the improved performance of the Il-96-300 over the Il-86 was the newer technology Aviadvigatel PS-90A turbofans. These 35,275-pound-thrust engines were more reliable and fuel efficient than the Kuznetsov NK-86s used on the first Soviet wide-body. Here an Il-96-300 of Aeroflot Russian International Airlines displays its double-slotted flaps and full-span leading-edge slats on final approach to Moscow's Sheremetyevo airport.

535 engines developed for the Boeing 757. Not surprisingly, the PS-90 also ended up powering the Tupolev Tu-204, Russia's answer to the 757. The PS-90 was the last engine designed under the leadership of Soloviev, the general designer for whom the bureau was named. The Soloviev Design Bureau later became part of a larger group and is today known as the Aviadvigatel Design Bureau. The first ll-96-300 flew from Khodinka on September 28, 1988, and eventually entered service in mid-1993.

Production of the Il-96-300 was very slow, however, and by the start of 1996 only five had been delivered to Aeroflot-Russian International Airlines (ARIA). Furthermore, the airline was disappointed with the new aircraft's higher-than-expected fuel consumption and lack of power. Ilyushin could see this coming and, some years earlier, began negotiations with Western enginemakers to power a stretched Il-96-300 version dubbed the -350 because it would nominally carry 350 passengers. This ultimately became the Il-96M and was to be powered by P&W's PW2337 engine, a derivative of the powerplant for the Boeing 757 and McDonnell Douglas C-17.

Ilyushin began by cutting up the Il-96-300 prototype and inserting two plugs to stretch the fuselage by 28 feet. The Il-96M, now almost 210 feet long with seating for up to 386 in a single class, made its public debut at the design bureau's Moscow site on March 30, 1993. The aircraft's maiden flight came a week later. It flew for 57 minutes on an extended ferry flight from Moscow City airport to the Zhukowsky flight-test center. The aircraft also incorporated Western-made avionics from Rockwell Collins, and together with the potential of the more reliable P&W engines, made the Il-96M an attractively priced wide-body for former Soviet airlines. At the time of the first flight, Ilyushin had letters of intent for around 30 aircraft from ARIA, Uzbekistan Airways, and Far East Aviation. Later that year, a Netherlands-based trading and leasing company, Partnairs NV, signed a similar letter for five firm and five options.

In January 1996, with the first production aircraft yet to fly, the U.S. Ex-Im (export-import) bank received U.S. government approval to lend $1 billion to the Russian airline ARIA. This was to pay the U.S. companies Collins and P&W for the avionics and engines on the 20 aircraft they had on order. At first, Boeing and

Not many aircraft get to be shown at different international air shows in different guises, but the prototype Il-96M was one. This aircraft originally appeared as the shorter Il-96-300 at the 1989 Paris air show but was then converted and stretched by 28 feet into the prototype Il-96M. The 209-foot-long jetliner was the first Russian wide-body to be powered by Western engines, in this case P&W PW2337s, and is pictured here performing a fly-past at the 1994 Farnborough air show.

McDonnell Douglas objected because they felt it created unfair competition for their airliners, particularly in developing markets such as China and India. In the end, the deal went through after ARIA agreed to set up an offshore registered company through which the Ex-Im bank could repossess the aircraft if the airline defaulted on payments. The Russian government also agreed to remove any trade barriers against the import of American-made jetliners.

Ilyushin's idea of extracting new long-range performance by shrinking the Il-86 and making the Il-96-300 was not new. Boeing and Lockheed both tried the concept in the 1970s, with varying degrees of success. The 747SB, or Short Body, was Boeing's response to a long-range requirement from Pan Am, which was on the verge of buying the heavyweight DC-10-30 to

The prototype Il-96M pictured shortly after takeoff from the Zhukovsky Flight Research Center in 1993. Note the large right-rudder deflection as the big jetliner comes around for a fly-past at the Mosaero show.

meet its needs. After much debate, Boeing decide to reduce the basic 747 fuselage by cutting its overall length by 47 feet, 1 inch. The SB, or "Sutter's balloon" (as it was nicknamed after its main conceptual father, Joe Sutter), was later rechristened SP, for Special Performance, by the hard-pushed Boeing marketing department.

The 747SP was not, however, just a simple shrink. It incorporated a structurally lighter wing, simpler flaps, and a 10-foot-wider horizontal tail span to maintain good pitch control and stability with the shorter body. Complex aerodynamic calculations and tests were conducted on the wing-body join, which was faired over with a new shape. The tip of the vertical tail was also increased by 5 feet, and the rudder was double-hinged. The main driving force behind most of these changes was a determined effort to make the 747SP handle exactly like its bigger brother. This would enable current 747 pilots to quickly and painlessly convert to the 276-seater, reducing training requirements and easing entry into service. The 747SP could fly up to 6,650 nautical miles with a full payload, reaching a previously unattained standard cruise altitude of 45,000 feet. Although the high altitudes were beneficial in terms of smooth air and uncongested airspace, the unexpectedly dry atmosphere caused dehydration among crew and passengers alike, forcing the use of humidifiers.

In the end, only 45 747SPs were built. Some said the project proved Boeing should stick to its more successful policy of stretching aircraft. It successfully stretched every standard-body it built, including the 757, and by 1997 with the cancellation of the 747-500 and -600, the 747 was the only Boeing jetliner never to have been stretched. However, some at Boeing believe the 747SP was a vital part of the wide-body story because it not only opened up new ultra-long-range routes, thereby helping to accelerate the development of the 747-400, but it also helped expose new airlines to the aircraft family and, therefore, led indirectly to more sales of the 747-200, -300 and, ultimately, -400.

Lockheed's long-range ambitions for the TriStar had been frustrated for several years by its own 1970 financial crisis stemming from cost-overruns on the C-5A Galaxy and other military programs, plus the collapse of its engine supplier, Rolls-Royce. Although Rolls reemerged as a virtually nationalized British company, long-range work was held up by the deep depression of the airline industry following the 1973 fuel crisis. Furthermore, the pace of growth was constrained by the speed at which Rolls-Royce could coax more power out of the RB.211 engine.

Early plans included a long-range TriStar called the Dash 8 to compete with the DC-10-30 and -40. The Dash 8 was killed by Lockheed's financial crisis and the cancellation of a projected 50,000-pound-thrust version of the RB.211 called the -61. Lockheed did proceed with development of heavier and more capable L-1011s including the TriStar 100 and 200 but was still haunted by the competitive specter of McDonnell Douglas's long-range DC-10-30 and -40. Lockheed even planned a version called

The 747SP looks particularly short and stubby from the side. The SP is 47 feet, 1 inch shorter than the standard 747 and was the only Boeing jetliner to have been deliberately shrunk rather than stretched (even the relatively short Boeing 720 was longer than the Dash 80 prototype). This Chinese-operated SP was delivered in 1980.

The Il-96M wing is common to the shorter Il-96-300 and is the most advanced ever developed for a large Russian-built transport. Swept at a relatively modest 30 degrees, the "aft-loaded," or supercritical, design is evident in the slightly scooped-out underside of the wing near the trailing edge. The vertical tail is more sharply swept at 45 degrees while the tailplane has the same sweep angle as the wing of a 747, some 37 degrees, 30 minutes.

the TriStar 2LR, later called the 250, as a long-range successor to the abandoned Dash 8. This was considered for purchase by Aeroflot of Russia, among others, and could have led to the setting up of TriStar and RB.211 production lines in Russia, but was vetoed by the U.S. Congress.

In mid-1975 British Airways was on the hunt for a replacement for its long-haul fleet of 707s and VC-10s. At the same time Lockheed conceived the idea of a shortened TriStar as an ideal 707 replacement. The aircraft, called the TriStar 500, was shortened by 20 feet, 2 inches and had space for a further 22,000 pounds of fuel, which was created in the center section. Compared to the TriStar 1,

▲ The long-range capability of the SP continues to keep the aircraft attractive. This brightly liveried jetliner was delivered to South African Airways in January 1977 and leased to Air Namibia, which used it to fly nonstop, long-haul routes such as London to Windhoek. The taller tail fin, which was extended 5 feet for the SP, is evident in this view as the aircraft lines up for take-off from London Heathrow.

▼ The TriStar 500 had an extended wingspan of 164 feet, 4 inches to improve long-range-cruise performance. However, the larger wings also had a greater amount of bend, so Lockheed developed "active ailerons" to compensate. The active control system reduced bending, and therefore, increased fatigue life. The more responsive ailerons also gave the -500 a much smoother ride through turbulence, providing what is known as gust alleviation.

the -500 carried 54,000 pounds more fuel. BA launched the program by converting orders for six TriStar 1s to -500s in August 1976 amid great optimism at Lockheed, which saw the new version as the beginning of a long-awaited revival in its war against the DC-10. At the time it forecast a market estimated at 244 TriStar 500s through 1985. Unfortunately for Lockheed, this was not to be the case. The -500 was to be the last type of TriStar made, and only 50 were built by the time production ended in 1983.

The L-1011-500 incorporated some novel features, including a computerized automatic performance-management system, the forerunner of the more modern digital flight management system. The wing-fuselage fillet was also redesigned to save weight, rather than drag, and to avoid producing some very awkwardly shaped cargo doors in the shortened rear fuselage.

▼ The "Frisbee" fairing below the tail-engine intake is clearly shown in this head-on view of a Delta TriStar 500. The fairing reduced the noise in the aft cabin while another new feature of the -500, a revised wing-to-body fairing, reduced drag.

Possibly the most notable external feature was a "Frisbee Fairing" beneath the center engine inlet. Named after its designer, Lockheed chief engineer Lloyd Frisbee, the fairing dramatically cut down an aerodynamic source of noise that had plagued earlier aircraft. This was traced to air stagnating at the fairing between the inlet and the fuselage. The new device was sharp-lipped and cleaved the air more efficiently than the original bluff fairing, which looked more like the bow of a super tanker. In efforts to stimulate more interest, later -500s were developed with extended wing tips and actively controlled ailerons, and earlier models were retrofitted with these updates.

New Twins on the Block

The pioneering twin-engined Airbus A300, together with continued improvements in turbofan power and reliability, convinced many of the doubters that big twins were not only safe but were also destined to be the most efficient wide-bodies of the future.

The first Boeing wide-body twin was the 767. The roots of the twin jet go back to the "7X7," which was a so-called "semi

▲ Pistols at dawn! Boeing's answer to the Airbus twin-jet series was the 767. Both the A310 and 767 were developed at roughly the same time and competed aggressively against each other for the same market. In this case, the aircraft in the distance is a Pan Am-operated A300 while the twin jet nearest the camera is an American Airlines 767-200.

wide-body" short-to-medium-range study aircraft capable of carrying around 200 passengers. The aircraft was aimed mainly at the U.S. majors, to fill the gap between larger tri-jets such as the DC-10 and smaller aircraft such as the 727-200 and the 7N7, which was designed to replace it. (The 7N7 ultimately became the 757 and opened up an entirely new market niche.) In Europe it would compete with the slightly larger A300. When the study began in 1972, the fuselage diameter was expected to be around 15 feet, 8 inches, but by 1975 had grown to 16 feet, 6 inches, which was the size of the 767 fuselage when finally launched. It had also reverted to a tri-jet by this stage, with either the new GE CFM56 engine or P&W's proposed JT10D. Deliberation continued as the 7X7 changed back from three to two engines, with pressure for a twin coming from Delta Air Lines and Western. United Air Lines, with its usual high-altitude Denver considerations, still favored a tri-jet.

By early 1978 the world market had recovered from the mid-1970s fuel crisis "blues" period, and Boeing felt optimistic enough to make firm proposals for a new-technology twin-

engined family that included a 180-seat 767-100 and a larger 210-seat 767-200. By mid-year the configurations were firm, and on July 14 the 767-200 was launched with an order for 30 from United Air Lines. Two more large orders quickly followed from American and Delta, which had so strongly influenced its twin configuration. The 767-100 was never built, but a stretched version, the 767-300, was later launched in 1983 and dramatically extended the life of the 767 program.

The final 767 design that first flew in September 1981 revealed some slightly unexpected developments. The fuselage, for example, was sized for a seven-across seating arrangement, one fewer than its nearest rival, at that time called the Airbus A300B10. However, Boeing defended the cross-section saying the "not-so-wide" wide-body was the preferred option for its largely domestic U.S. customers and meant that 80 percent of passengers would use window and aisle seats, rather than the deeply unpopular center seat. Its aerodynamic analysis also suggested that the slim-line body would save up to 2 percent more fuel per trip compared to a slightly wider design. The fuselage, as usual for a Boeing design, was composed of the familiar double-bubble, with the floor level arranged just below halfway to give almost vertical cabin sidewalls. Although this improved cabin dimensions, the under-floor space was reduced, requiring the use of smaller LD-2 freight containers.

The wing was the first application of supercritical design on a Boeing wide-body. As the thicker, flat-topped wing

One of the pioneers of ETOPS was Israeli flag-carrier El Al. One of the airline's 767-200 aircraft, delivered in July 1983, is pictured on final approach in landing configuration. Note the peace symbol displayed prominently by the flight-deck windows.

enjoyed the benefit of much-delayed supersonic-shock-wave onset, the designers could get away with a modest wing-sweep angle of 31.5 degrees for a normal cruise speed of Mach 0.8. The deep wing could easily accommodate a complex set of flaps and slats, as well as some 16,700 gallons of fuel. This was later raised to a maximum of more than 24,000 gallons. The big wing was 3,050 square feet in area, providing good high-altitude performance and, more important, allowed Boeing to stretch the 767 with ease.

Ironically, the 767's closest rival, the A310, was also given the go-ahead in July 1978 on the basis of commitments from Air France, Lufthansa, and Swissair. Airbus planned a family of wide-body twins from the very beginning and by the mid-'70s was working on a shortened version of the A300 known by the project name A300B10. Everything about the original plan was simple. The aircraft would be 14 frames shorter than the A300 but with the same wing and tail. However, the program faced huge uncertainty. At one point a potential joint effort was considered with arch-rival Boeing under the projected title A300BB10, the extra "B" standing

for Boeing. Questions were also raised over the economic sense of putting a shorter fuselage on an unmodified A300 wing.

As a result, the idea of an all-new wing was born, and by October 1977, two wing options were being looked at: A brand-new design and a modified version building on the existing wing box. Airbus finally selected the all-new wing that, like the wing of the A300, was built by British Aerospace. The design differed from the first airfoil in being much thicker where the wing joined the fuselage, with a sharp taper upward from the wing root to the lower inboard wing surface. This produced a distinct dihedral-shaped area with a large volume for fuel and guaranteed a more than adequate margin for ground clearance for the big turbofans, which were hung further inboard than on the A300 and further out from the leading edge. The deeper root depth also gave more structural strength and reduced interference drag at high Mach numbers.

The A310 was also the first wide-body to use wing-tip fences or devices, which improved the efficiency of the airfoil by reducing drag, cutting lift loss at the tip and decreasing fuel burn. This small device became more familiar as Boeing and McDonnell Douglas adopted the "winglet," a more extreme version of the same technology for the 747 and MD-11, respectively. Winglets work by extracting energy from the airflow that forms the vortices that stream from the wing. These vortices are generated when low-pressure air from the upper surface of the wing tip mixes with higher pressure air from below the wing. The two streams powerfully intertwine, slowing the aircraft and, during final approach to landing, causing dangerous spinning air currents, or vortices, in the wake of the aircraft. The winglet dissipates much of this energy, improving wing performance and destroying the potentially dangerous vortices.

The A310 was initially offered in two main versions, a -100 version aimed at 2,000-nautical-mile routes and a -200 version for 3,000-nautical-mile routes. As it turned out, the aircraft quickly became known as an excellent long-range aircraft, and while sales of the -200 mushroomed, no airlines selected the -100. Airlines found that the A310 was a good 707 or DC-8 replacement and perfect for long "thin" routes that would not fill up a wide-body tri-jet or a 747. Ultimately, a -300 version

was developed that could carry 220 passengers up to 5,200 nautical miles. The range performance of the -200 was also eventually stretched to 3,650 nautical miles with a load of 220 passengers in a typical two-class layout.

Both the A310 and 767 had a profound, if unexpected, effect on the air-transport business. Both were introduced by their manufacturers as medium-, or short-range transports but ended up making a huge impact on the long-range over-water routes around the world. By the mid-1990s, for example, twins dominated the busiest international long-haul routes in the world across the North Atlantic, displacing even the mighty 747. Consistent engine reliability and all-around safety led to both being granted the status of ETOPS. This meant that the aircraft

▶ Although selected only by British Airways and one Chinese airline, the Rolls-Royce RB.211-524G turbofan is the most powerful engine option available on the 767 with a thrust rating of 60,600 pounds. The stretched -300 proved to be the most popular version of the 767 and by 1997 the only -200 airframes being produced were for military derivatives.

▼ Boeing's tradition of stretching its aircraft continued with the 767 which was extended by 21 feet to create the -300. The extra length is clearly evident in this view of an Alitalia aircraft awaiting delivery from Boeing's Everett site in 1995. The aircraft was U.K., and not Italian registered, to allow Alitalia to operate the new aircraft without being affected by an air-crew strike that was going on at the time.

▲ Further stretches of the 767 continued to be studied, and by early 1997 Boeing launched a new variant dubbed the -400. The extra-long 767 accommodated about 20 percent more passengers, or roughly 40 more seats, but was otherwise unchanged from the -300; it even used the same engines. The extra length required changes to the undercarriage and some strengthening of the wing and fuselage skin and structure, but changes were generally kept to a minimum to keep the cost down. The study interested several major U.S. airlines, including Delta and American, one of whose 767-300s is pictured here on final approach.

could legally fly on routes that were up to three hours flying time away from a diversionary airfield on just one engine.

The ETOPS explosion overturned the long-haul imperative of needing three or four engines. With 180-minute ETOPS clearance in the bag, operators could fly the smaller and cheaper twins on long-haul routes that would have been impossible to sustain, let alone make a profit on, with a larger jetliner. Myriad new destinations opened up, and frequencies on traditional routes grew. Whole new route structures emerged with more direct services between city pairs that previously were only linked via major international gateways such as New York and London.

Airbus built on its twin-jet ETOPS advantage by developing a newer, longer-range version of the A300 called the -600R. The jetliner featured many of the advances developed for the later twins including the A310 rear fuselage, which does not taper as quickly as the original A300's. This allows the A300-600R to hold more passengers without having to dramatically increase the length of the aircraft. The -600R was also fitted with the two-crew glass cockpit of later models and had a lot more composite materials in the primary and secondary structure to save weight. The design was announced in December 1980, and the first P&W JT9D-powered A300-600R flew almost exactly three years later. The first GE CF6-80C2-powered version flew in 1985, and one year later the first A300-600R with PW4000s made its first flight. By 1990 the P&W-engined A300-600R had proved itself trouble-free and worthy of 120-minute ETOPS operations. Approval was given by the European authorities in 1990, and the go-ahead for full 180-minute ETOPS was received the following year. Similar clearances for the GE version were obtained by 1994.

New Look, Old Style

By the mid-1980s, the rising tide of new technology that swept into the industry with the new twin jets gave rise to anoth-

The "semi wide-body" cross section of the 767 is clearly shown in this nose-on view of a Britannia Airways aircraft as it waits for takeoff. The 767 proved to be a "jack-of-all-trades," being not only popular with long-haul international scheduled airlines but also with the European charter market. This aircraft is named *Bobby Moore OBE* in honor of the captain of the English soccer team that won the World Cup in 1966.

A new compact wing was designed for the A310. The traditional low-speed aileron at the end of the wing was deleted and roll control was exercised by small all-speed trailing-edge ailerons and electrically signaled spoilers. The three outermost sections in this picture are the roll-control spoilers, but these only open on the down-going wing. Each is controlled by a digital flight control system via two computers, each with its own software for redundancy. The inboard sections serve as air brakes, and all 14 surfaces pop up on landing to reduce lift on the wing. Note the wing-tip device, which has a vertical span of 55 inches and reduces fuel burn in the cruise by more than 1.5 percent.

Airbus continued to make major headway into markets that had previously been the sole domain of the U.S. majors Boeing and Douglas. The A310 was at the forefront of the attack as it provided a very economical long-range solution for some of the "thinner" routes between Europe and some of the less-popular gateways that opened up in the United States as more and more ETOPS routes were inaugurated. Here, a Delta A310-300, formerly belonging to Pan Am, taxies in toward the gate at London Gatwick.

Another trans-Atlantic twin-jet pioneer was Wardair of Canada. The airline has now disappeared, and this A310 is used by the Canadian Armed Forces as a tanker-transport.

The deep gulled wing of the A310 is illustrated to good effect in this view of an Emirates -300 as it is pushed back from the gate at Dubai to begin yet another flight. Although the new wing was structurally simpler than the regular A300 wing, the complex curves on the underside of the wing required new machines to form the skin. The drag-reducing wing-tip device is also shown clearly. Note the faired-in wing-tip navigation light.

er generation of wide-bodies. While the technology of the engines, avionics, and flight-deck displays was new, the basic designs were not, and both Boeing and McDonnell Douglas took advantage of the developments to launch radically updated versions of existing jetliners.

Boeing announced the design go-ahead of a new-generation 747, the -400, in July 1985 and flew it less than three years later. The 747-400 was based structurally on the stretched-upper-deck 747-300 but was otherwise a major leap from previous generations. Externally, the only giveaway was an increase of 12 feet in wingspan and the addition of large winglets extravagantly swept at 60 degrees. The winglets also canted outward by 22 degrees, although this increased by a degree or two when the aircraft was fully loaded with fuel and sitting on the ground, thereby temporarily increasing span by a few feet!

In efforts to cut back weight, many advanced materials were introduced on the 747. Advanced aluminum alloys used in the wing box area saved 6,000 pounds. Composites were used for winglets, main-deck floor panels, cabin fittings, and in engine nacelles. Most of the major changes were reserved for inside the cockpit where the flight engineer's position was eliminated by a radical flight-deck redesign. Standard instruments were replaced by six cathode-ray-tube (CRT) displays, helping to cut the number of lights, switches, and gauges by around 600.

The radical revamp of the -400 variant gave the 747 a new lease on life. Despite giving Boeing some major production and development headaches, the aircraft rapidly matured, and more than 530 had been ordered by 1997, representing over half of the total 747 production run.

McDonnell Douglas embarked on a very similar but somewhat more ambitious upgrade of its DC-10, making it capable of taking a higher payload over long-distance routes. After many false starts, including an abandoned DC-10-61, -62, -63, and a completely different tri-jet concept called the MD-100, the MD-11 design was finalized in late 1985. The most instantly visible changes from the DC-10 included an 18-foot, 7-inch stretch of the fuselage and the addition of large winglets. However, as on the 747-400, much of the change had been wrought beneath the skin. The flight deck was one of the most advanced yet developed, with six large CRT displays made by Honeywell. Like the 747-400's, the MD-11's cockpit could be operated by just two crew members. The engines were fitted with sophisticated electronics that could control power and overall performance more precisely than any human could.

The new tri-jet promised much more capability than the DC-10 and attracted a lot of interest, particularly from loyal Douglas customers of past generations such as American, Delta, Alitalia, Finnair, and KLM. The program got the go-ahead in December 1986, and after some production holdups, the first aircraft finally flew on January 10, 1990, eight months later than expected. Five MD-11s flew almost 2,000 hours in a tight certification effort that was rewarded with an airworthiness ticket by the end of November that year.

Despite its best efforts to get the MD-11 on track, McDonnell Douglas almost immediately discovered a shortfall in performance. The aircraft could not meet its performance guarantees, mainly because the GE and P&W engines were too fuel-thirsty. Together with the enginemakers, the company embarked on a four-year-long "get-well" program that covered everything from squeezing every drop of performance from the engines to cutting aircraft weight and reducing drag. The performance-improvement program, or PIP, eventually produced a worthy 8 percent improvement in performance, producing a range of more than 7,000 nautical miles with 298 passengers and baggage. Though this was in excess of the original performance specification, McDonnell Douglas felt the PIP was a vital part of efforts to keep the aircraft attractive. Several airlines and leasing companies canceled or reduced orders as news of the performance problems coincided with the onset of a bad industry recession.

By 1995 McDonnell Douglas had achieved a remarkable turnaround. Seemingly once on the brink of closing, the troubled tri-jet program improved because of the PIPs, and new sales slowly began to trickle in. Some were for an extended-range version, the MD-11ER, which was offered with extra fuel capacity and seats for 323 passengers; range was increased to 7,210 nautical miles. The freighter version, which had first been ordered by Federal Express, particularly aroused new interest.

▼ The red-painted winglet of this Virgin Atlantic 747 is the only significant external clue that this is a -400 series, the most popular version of the aircraft yet developed by Boeing. Sharp-eyed observers might also notice that the wing-to-body fairing design was altered to improve cruise efficiency, though some late-build -200s and -300s were also fitted with the redesigned fairing. Note the enormous triple-slotted flaps which are fully extended for landing. This Virgin aircraft is named *Lady Penelope* in memory of a popular British TV children's program called *Thunderbirds*. The program's catch phrase was "F.A.B.," hence the 747's registration: G-VFAB.

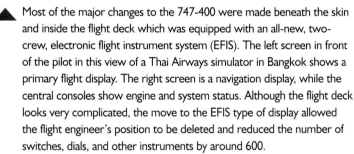 Most of the major changes to the 747-400 were made beneath the skin and inside the flight deck which was equipped with an all-new, two-crew, electronic flight instrument system (EFIS). The left screen in front of the pilot in this view of a Thai Airways simulator in Bangkok shows a primary flight display. The right screen is a navigation display, while the central consoles show engine and system status. Although the flight deck looks very complicated, the move to the EFIS type of display allowed the flight engineer's position to be deleted and reduced the number of switches, dials, and other instruments by around 600.

Like Boeing with the 747, Douglas looked to the wing tips to produce an improvement for the MD-11. The wingspan was increased over the DC-10-30 by 4 feet, 6 inches with the addition of Whitcomb-style winglets (named after NASA Langley research engineer Richard T. Whitcomb, who is credited with much of the pioneering concept work on both the supercritical wing and the winglet). These were canted outward and extended 7 feet above the wing and 2 feet, 6 inches below.

However, later orders for MD-11Fs from Lufthansa, which announced orders and options for 12 in 1996, only briefly prolonged the life of the tri-jet which war expecked to be phased out with the Boeing take over.

Hi-Tech Wide-Bodies

Airbus had long intended to compete with Boeing and McDonnell Douglas on the large-capacity medium-, long-, and very-long-range sectors. This came to fruition with the A330 and A340. The two were so alike in virtually every detail that Airbus treated them as one program. Remarkably, the two had the same fuselage, cockpit, and wing. The only major difference was in the number and type of engines. The A330, as a medium- or long-range airliner, was designed to be powered by two powerful high-bypass-ratio turbofans, while the long-range A340 would feature four engines rated at around half the power, each.

The two originated as the A300B9 and B11, the B10 eventually becoming the A310. By 1980, they had become the twin-aisle TA9 and TA11 and did not assume the titles A330 and A340 until January 1986, when the Airbus Supervisory Board announced that the aircraft were almost defined and could be discussed with "potential customer airlines." The A330 was projected as a 5,800-nautical-mile-range airliner for around 308 passengers, powered by two big CF6-80C2 or PW4000 turbofans. The A340 was aimed at the longer-range routes (up to 6,700 nautical miles) and could carry 261 passengers. It would be powered by either CFM56-5 made by the GE-Snecma company CFM International (CFMI) or by the V2500 made by International Aero Engines (IAE).

Although it was still the early days of the program, two factors began to concern Airbus: the threat posed by the MD-

11 and the fact that the CFM56 engine on offer for the A340 was already close to its power limits on takeoff. Airbus was therefore delighted when IAE proposed an engine called the V2500 SuperFan, which offered more than 30,000 pounds of thrust and up to 17 percent lower fuel consumption. The SuperFan demonstrated a radical approach to future engine design and consisted of a large fan that was driven by a gearbox attached to the core. The fan blades resembled those found on much-larger turbofans used on the Boeing 777 of the late 1990s and could be controlled in pitch.

The promise of the SuperFan gave the A340 a sudden edge over the MD-11, and Airbus redefined the aircraft in two versions. The A340-200 would be capable of carrying 262 passengers across ranges in excess of 7,850 nautical miles. A longer A340-300, stretched by 14 feet, would be able to carry 295 passengers over 7,000 nautical miles. CFM International retaliated by offering a more ambitious development of the CFM56-5A1, the -5C1, which could produce 30,600 pounds of thrust. Airbus offered both engines, and on January 15, 1987, Lufthansa said it would commit to the SuperFan-powered A340 with orders and options for 30. Within two months, Northwest Airlines

▼ Early MD-11 long-range performance was plagued by excessively thirsty engines. A major effort by Douglas to reduce drag, coupled with engine "get-well" programs, brought dramatic improvements in range performance. Beneficiaries included China Eastern, whose MD-11 is seen lifting off from Seattle's Runway 34 Right, bound for Shanghai, China. Note the center main wheels have lifted off slightly before the main wheels.

▼ Despite the drag and fuel-burn improvements, airline confidence in the MD-11 was badly dented by its performance problems. The freighter version, however, became more popular as time went on, and Federal Express became a staunch supporter. However, the loss of market confidence and high costs were blamed for the 1996 decision by McDonnell Douglas not to go ahead with a planned rewinged, stretched MD-11 dubbed the MD-XX. This decision, plus some notable military contract losses later the same year, had even more shattering repercussions for the company. In December 1996, Boeing and McDonnell Douglas announced a merger.

signed a letter of intent for 20 A340s and 10 A330s but, significantly, did not announce an engine choice. Then, in mid-April, IAE dropped a bombshell and announced that it would not be making the SuperFan engine.

The news shocked Lufthansa and came as a body blow to Airbus. Of course, it delighted CFMI, which realized it suddenly had a monopoly on the A340 with the CFM56. International Aero Engines said it had decided not to offer the futuristic powerplant because it "was felt premature to launch the SuperFan program at this stage, in the light of the technical program risks

▲ By 1997 it became likely that, following the merger with Boeing, the ultimate Douglas-built long-haul jetliner was the extended-range version of the MD-11. The first, and one of the few MD-11ERs built, was this aircraft for World Airways. The aircraft is pictured on a predelivery test flight over the California coastline. *McDonnell Douglas*

▼ An outstanding development of the MD-11 from the beginning was the all-new, two-crew, digital EFIS flight deck. Dominated by six Honeywell-made 8 x 8-inch CRT displays, the flight deck was widely held to be one of the most advanced in the industry up to and including the 777. Advanced features include an automated aircraft-system control, which replaced the flight engineer's function and which was located above the crew on an overhead panel. The engines were also manipulated by electronic controls and the aircraft was fitted with a longitudinal stability augmentation system (LSAS), which compensated for the aircraft's smaller horizontal stabilizers. McDonnell Douglas

of meeting an entry-into-service date of spring 1992 to satisfy the airlines' desires."

Airbus quickly regrouped. Its problem: How to boost the performance of the CFM56-powered A340 to match that promised by the SuperFan version. The answer came in two stages. First, Airbus redesigned the A340 wing (and therefore that of the identical A330) with a larger span of 192 feet, 3 inches—almost 10 feet extra. It replaced the A310 type of wing fences with more-prominent 9-foot winglets. Second, CFMI came up with more power from the engine and produced the 31,200-pound-thrust CFM56-5C2. By 1995, it was able to offer a 34,000-pound-thrust engine, the CFM56-5C4.

Final go-ahead for the combined program was given at the 1987 Paris air show, by which time Airbus had received commitments for 60 A340s and 38 A330s. Over the next year, the A330 design was stretched by almost 4 feet to make the fuselage the same length as the longer A340-300's. The wing and glass cockpit were also defined, the six-screen electronic flight-instrument display and general layout being virtually identical to the flight deck of the A320. Like their little twin-jet sibling, the A330 and A340 were fitted with fly-by-wire flight controls and side-stick controllers rather than conventional yokes.

Four engines provide wing-bending-moment relief for the heavier, longer-range A340. Airbus believed that, even though it was the same wing, the design would be not compromised by using two larger engines to provide similar bending relief for the medium-range A330 at slightly lower take-off weights. *Airbus Industrie*

The A330/340 wing is 40 percent bigger than the A300 wing, with a span of 197 feet, 10 inches. Like other giant jetliners of its age, it has winglets, in this case 9 feet tall. The advanced "aft-loaded" cross-section is clearly visible in this picture of a Virgin A340 preparing for take-off with flaps and slats set.

Around the same time, the A330 became the first Airbus to be offered with a choice from all three of the major enginemakers. Agreements were signed with P&W covering the PW4164/4168 and with Rolls-Royce for the RB.211-524L (later known as the Trent 700). At the time, the A330 was already committed to a version of the GE CF6-80C2, which later became known as the CF6-80E1.

The higher demand for the A340 accelerated its development ahead of the A330. The A340-300 became the first of the new family to take to the air on October 25, 1991. The first flight of the shorter A340-200 took place the following April, while the first A330, the tenth on the joint production line, flew on November 2, 1992.

The program encountered more than its fair share of problems. Early flight-test results showed the performance of the A340 was poorer than predicted, requiring remedial action from Airbus and CFMI. Aerodynamic and engine improvements were hurriedly introduced, and the performance improved. At the same time, however, it was discovered that the airframe was lighter than expected and the big wing could hold more fuel than predicted. This unexpected bonus was later offset slightly when the A330 wing failed in the static test rig. The failure was traced to a weakness in the rear spar, which was traced to loads that would only be experienced on the twin-engined A330 rather than the four-engined A340. As a result, the required modifications proved not as extensive as had first been feared.

The A340 received European certification on December 22, 1992, after a 750-flight, 2,400-hour flight-test program involv-

Kuwait Airways rebuilt after the invasion by Iraq that destroyed or scattered its fleet. One of its major purchases was a fleet of A340s, one of which is pictured here with flaps and slats extended for landing. Daimler-Benz Aerospace makes the carbon-fiber fin for the A330/340 which is identical to the fin on the A300-600 and A310. The horizontal tail, built by CASA of Spain, is also very similar to the A300/A310 unit and includes a fuel tank which is drained or filled to help trim the aircraft for the best angle to improve cruise efficiency.

ing six aircraft. The first aircraft, a shorter A340-200, was turned over to Lufthansa in the winter of 1993. The German airline became the first to use the A340 for revenue service on March 15, 1993, when it flew its first aircraft on a scheduled flight from Frankfurt to Newark. Air France took first delivery of the A340-300, on February 26, 1993.

The A330 was certified simultaneously by the U.S. and European authorities on October 21, 1993, after a yearlong, 1,100-hour flight-test program. At the very end of that year Air Inter, the French operator, took delivery of the first A330, and on January 14, 1994, the big twin carried its first fare-paying passengers on a flight between Paris and Marseilles. The P&W PW4168-powered A330 followed close behind, though its introduction into service was held up because of problems with the thrust reversers.

On June 30, 1994, the test program suffered a serious blow when a PW4000-powered A330 crashed at Blagnac Airport in Toulouse, killing all seven test personnel aboard. Crew error was later blamed for the accident which occurred as they were testing for a new autopilot setting. The test involved flying at minimum

Unless you look very closely, this could be the uncluttered flight deck of either an A330 or an A340. Note the absence of traditional control columns and the presence, instead, of sidestick controllers similar to those used in Lockheed Martin F-16 fighter. This flight deck, along with the sidesticks, was introduced with the narrow-body A320. The number of throttle levers indicates this is an A340. Without the control column in the way, the crew can now pull out a chart table from its stowage area under the flight-deck displays.

The clean lines of an LTU A330 captured in flight over France on a predelivery test. *Airbus Industrie*

An Airbus A330 demonstrator shows off its agility at the Dubai air show in 1993. In normal flight, the bank angle is limited to 33 degrees when in autopilot or 67 degrees with the stick fully over to one side. Just visible between the closing doors of the main undercarriage is the square panel covering the optional center-gear position.

speed with the center of gravity as far back as possible and with maximum climb angle and one engine at idle power to simulate a failure. The inquiry also highlighted the need to closely monitor the speed of the A330 during autopilot and altitude operations.

Despite the crash and some problems with the engines' thrust reversers, the effort continued, and Thai Airways International became the first airline to receive the P&W-powered A330 on December 12, 1994, and put it into revenue service a week later. Meanwhile, the Rolls-Royce Trent 700-powered A330 became the first Airbus to be powered by the British enginemaker on January 31, 1994, when it made its maiden flight. It was certified by the end of the year and entered service with launch customer Cathay Pacific of Hong Kong on February 27, 1995.

In the midst of this hectic activity at Toulouse, Airbus was constantly checking on the progress of testing on another big twinjet program more than 5,000 miles away to the west. The big twin was the Boeing 777, which was only three months away from hand-over to launch customer United Air Lines. Another chapter in the battle of the giant jetliners was about to begin.

The use of digital, computer-aided-design systems is revolutionizing the manufacture of giant jetliners. Boeing introduced the IBM/Dassault-developed CATIA (computer-aided three-dimensional interactive applications) system for the 777 and achieved dramatic results. This CATIA image shows the flight deck viewed from the rear. The large red-colored cavity is the space for the nose-gear wheelwell. *Boeing*

Boeing's "incredibles" watch the fruit of their labor begin to come together inside the new factory at Everett as the first complete front fuselage (sections 41 and 42) are moved for final body join. It was only at this point that the sheer size of the first giant jetliner could really be grasped for the first time. Compare the rather hand-built, patchy look of airplane number one against the quality of more recent 747s (see p. 71). *Boeing*

LAND OF THE GIANTS

BUILDING GIANT JETLINERS IS ONE OF THE MOST COMPLEX
and challenging manufacturing tasks ever undertaken. To see Boeing's awesome assembly site at Everett, Washington, the largest-volume building in the world, or to watch the huge bulk of the Airbus Beluga landing with yet another cargo of aircraft wings or fuselage sections, gives some indication of the enormous scale of the enterprise.

However, the vast impact of the wide-body goes much deeper than this. It affects every aspect of manufacturing, from the size of the automated machines to the area of the factory floor. The growing scale and scope of each project demanded larger supplier networks. For Boeing, Lockheed, and McDonnell Douglas, these were predominantly national but gradually grew to include suppliers in virtually every corner of the world. Airbus, by its very nature as a pan-European group, was international from the very start and created a model of worldwide organization.

Wide-Body Capital

Boeing started the ball rolling when it began hunting for a place to build the giant C-5A airlifter for the USAF in late 1964. It had large facilities at Renton, close to Seattle, and at nearby Boeing Field, but neither were anywhere near the size that it needed. More than 50 sites were considered, some close to home and others as far away as Marietta, Georgia, where the C-5A was ultimately built after Lockheed won the competition in 1965. Others were up and down California, as far south as San Diego and as far north as San Francisco, while other candidates included Denver, Cleveland, and the former Strategic Air Command base at Moses Lake, Washington.

New production methods were introduced with the 777, including this giant rotating gantry that turns the fuselage sections over to allow easier access for final assembly work to be completed.

Although the C-5A contract had been lost the previous August, the Boeing directors signaled the search for the site to continue when they gave the go-ahead for the 747 program in March 1966. Three months later, Boeing acquired 780 acres of mostly forest-covered ground adjacent to a small regional airport at Paine Field, some 30 miles north of Seattle. Immediately, the clock began ticking. The whole site had to be built and up and running to produce the first 747 in just 26 months!

The first priority was to build a railroad line to connect the site with the main line five miles away. The track bed was hacked out through rough terrain to climb up a steep 5.6 percent gradient to the edge of the plateau on which Paine Field was built. The northeast corner of the site, where Boeing wanted to build part of the massive plant, was littered with gullies and mounds. These had to be filled in, or leveled, whichever was appropriate, and rolled flat in double-quick time to meet the pressing deadline. Such was the pace of development that even as construction of the initial 200-million-cubic-foot building was in progress, production work was started. The construction gang vacated one area, and aircraft production workers, wearing hard hats, immediately moved in. Malcolm Stamper, the original vice president and general manager in charge of the 747, nicknamed his work force the "incredibles" for their pioneering work in very difficult working conditions.

Without the railroad, Boeing would quickly be out of business. A big proportion of all its jetliners arrive at the final-assembly site by a line that climbs up to Everett via the second-steepest incline (5.6 percent) in the U.S. The front end of a locomotive going upgrade is 3 feet higher than the rear wheels. Fuselage sections, including those stacked behind the receiving depot, and other large subassemblies gather here from all over the world. The large light-colored box in the middle bay is a center wing box which has arrived at Seattle by ship from Japan.

At the peak of development, Boeing was thought to be spending some $15 million a day. It was said that if the "incredibles" were just 10 percent "screwed up," then Boeing was losing $1 million a day. In all, the company spent $200 million on construction of the site, which by 1997 covered almost 99 acres and remains the largest industrial production area under a single roof. Upwards of $800 million more was spent on research and development, manpower, and new tooling. In addition, the various suppliers, including enginemaker P&W, spent roughly $500 million on the 747 program.

In January 1967, production operations for the 747 began at Everett, and the building was formally "activated" on May 1. By that date, parts were being fabricated and assembled in 49 states and in six other countries. Because of the sheer scale of the project and the speed at which it was scheduled to take place, Boeing was forced to subcontract more than 60 percent of the 747, a greater percentage than any previous aircraft. In all, around 1,500 prime suppliers and some 15,000 secondary suppliers were involved in bringing together more than 4,500,000 parts for the first aircraft.

The biggest parts or subassemblies produced outside Boeing included most of the fuselage, wing flaps and control surfaces, landing gear, tail, and engines. The fuselage sections, from just aft of the flight deck to the aft pressure bulkhead, were designed and made by Northrop's Norair Division at Hawthorne, near Los Angeles International Airport. Major sections were supplied by Vought Aircraft in Texas. Thirty years later, the same parts are still being made this way, though by 1996 both companies operated under the Northrop Grumman name. Today, a total of more than 40 subassembled panels (the largest measuring up to 30 x 20 feet) are delivered by rail to Everett for assembly into four major "barrel" sections. These are then bolted together to form the bulk of the fuselage. A nose section, made by Boeing's Wichita Division, is added to make the complete fuselage.

When it came to making the 767 some 13 years later, international involvement reached an unprecedented level. Choosing subcontractors took on new importance as internationally placed work became linked to the specific airlines buying the product. By far the biggest slice of the action in the wide-body twin-jet went to Japan, where three manufacturers (Fuji, Kawasaki, and Mitsubishi) made the wing fairings, main landing-gear doors, center body fuselage panels, exit hatches, wing in-spar ribs, rear fuselage body panels, stringers, passenger and cargo doors, and the dorsal fin. The Italian aerospace company Alenia also won a big part of the 767, making wing-control surfaces, flaps and leading-edge slats, wing tips, elevators, the fin, the rudder, and the nose radome. Bombardier of Canada was chosen to make the rear fuselage. Northrop Grumman again took the lion's share of the U.S.-based subcontractor work, making the wing center section and adjacent lower fuselage.

In the early 1990s, the Everett plant was again expanded to accommodate the 777. In all, Boeing spent around $1.5 billion on a massive expansion effort that virtually doubled the size of the already enormous factory to cover 64 acres. The factory was sized to handle a huge variety of production lines, which by 1997 already included lines for five major versions of the 767, two types of 747-400, and

Northrop Grumman-built fuselage sections, including a freight-door subassembly, are loaded into a rail car in Los Angeles before beginning a journey of more than 1,000 miles to the Everett plant.

two variants of the 777. Further juggling was required with the planned start of new 767 and 777 derivatives in the late 1990s.

Some 275,000 cubic yards of concrete were poured to form the floor area of the new production lines, enough to make 44 miles of four-lane freeway. The large, six-story-high buildings, built to the same basic design as the original 747 factory, required 85,000 tons of steel, or virtually twice the amount needed to erect the Empire State Building in New York City. The new buildings also included a sophisticated new paint hangar that incorporated massive air-filtering and air-scrubbing systems to ensure the facility met stiff environmental rules.

The scale of building work was matched on the inside with new, state-of-the-art tooling such as an automated wing-spar assembly machine to handle the 777's 105-foot main wing spars.

The proportion of outside subcontractors grew once more on the 777. The same three Japanese aerospace "majors" again took a large slice, in this case as part of a 20 percent share in the whole program. They were responsible for the fuselage panels, doors, wing center section, wing-to-body fairing, and wing in-spar ribs. Alenia again provided parts including the outboard wing flaps and radome. Embraer of Brazil supplied part of the wing tip and flaps structure. Aerospace Technologies of Australia and Hawker de Havilland provided the all-composite rudder and elevators, respectively. Short Brothers of Northern Ireland, a long-time specialist in engine pods for the Boeing line, supplied a nose-gear door, as did Singapore Aerospace. American suppliers again included Northrop Grumman, Rockwell (most of which was later bought by Boeing), Kaman Aerospace, and a host of smaller companies.

For the first time in any commercial aircraft program, every single supplier built its parts to a computer-based design provided on a worldwide database. The 777 was the first 100 percent paperless Boeing jetliner and was designed using the IBM/Dassault digital design system called the CATIA (computer-aided three-dimensional interactive applications). Using CATIA, all the designs were created using 3D solid images. The pieces were put together on the screen to see if they fit together exactly. Manufacturers anywhere around the globe could access the same database and instantly check to see that their part, or parts, were conforming to the specification.

Another innovation of the 777 program, and one that also paid dividends on later development efforts including the Next Generation 737, was the $370 million Integrated Aircraft Systems Lab (IASL). A large building was built near Boeing Field initially to support the 777 and was basically a giant simulator. Every single system on the aircraft was replicated exactly in the IASL to "smoke out" any problems that might otherwise have gone undiscovered until later, when they would have been far more costly to correct. The level of replication was so high that the IASL was nicknamed "aircraft zero," "777 No. 0," or "the skinless aircraft."

California Trijets

Like Boeing, Lockheed faced a space problem when it came to making its wide-body tri-jet, the L-1011 TriStar. The company's Burbank site in the San Fernando valley was used extensively for production of major subassemblies, as well as design and research, but simply could not accommodate the final assembly line of this giant jetliner.

After considering various other locations, Lockheed California selected Palmdale as the site for a brand-new factory. Sited in the high desert of Mojave, it was nevertheless relatively close to Burbank as the crow flies and was connected by the Antelope Valley freeway that punched through a convenient gap in the San Gabriel Mountains. An important factor was Palmdale's having two 12,000-foot runways, making it perfect for flight testing. Construction of the "Star Factory in the Desert," or "Plant 10" as it was otherwise called, began in mid-1968. The seven-building complex cost more than $50 million, almost $20 million more than originally estimated, and took two years to complete. Lockheed shelled out a further $60 million to expand production capacity at Burbank. Although TriStar production ended in 1983, the site became the focus for military activity and eventually was the new home of Lockheed Advanced Development Company, better known as the "Skunk Works," which moved there from Burbank in 1990. Following Lockheed's merger with Martin Marietta, the site later became known simply as Lockheed Martin Skunk Works.

The L-1011 was a more international project than either the 747 or DC-10 had been, thanks mainly to its exclusive use of Rolls-Royce RB.211 engines and Short Brothers engine nacelles. Canadian content was also extremely high. The auxiliary power unit (APU) and its accessories, air-conditioning, engine starting, fuselage assemblies, landing-gear doors, and flight simulator were all Canadian supplied. Bristol Aerospace of Winnipeg also provided the enormous S-shaped air-inlet duct for the tail engine. Other non-U.S. suppliers included Kawasaki Aircraft of Osaka, Japan, which was selected to build cabin and cargo doors.

Nashville-based Avco (later part of Textron Aerostructures) supplied most of the main wing structure, Menasco provided the beefy-looking landing gear, and Bertea (later part of Parker Bertea) supplied the "flying-tail" control system, which helped trim the aircraft and cut cruise drag. Other U.S. suppliers included Collins (later part of Rockwell), Sundstrand, BF Goodrich,

The gleaming nose (section 41) of a 747-400 is built by Boeing Wichita and is almost identical to the very first units that entered production 30 years ago.

Sperry (later part of Honeywell), Goodyear, and Lear Siegler (later part of GEC Marconi).

Not much farther to the south, McDonnell Douglas was in a better position to kick off production of its new DC-10. The newly created company was suddenly well placed to distribute the design, development, and manufacture of the tri-jet around different parts of the combined McDonnell and Douglas empire. Final assembly was set up at Long Beach, where the successful DC-8 family would soon be coming to the end of its production run. The wing design and development was handled by the aerodynamicists at McDonnell in St. Louis, where the company specialized in high-speed combat aircraft such as the F-4 Phantom and was soon to begin design work on the F-15 Eagle. Manufacture of the wings was the responsibility of Douglas at Long Beach. The company's Santa Monica site, which had spawned all the famous DC-series of piston-powered airliners, was still very active and was given the job of producing the nose section.

Section 41s receive attention. The two subassemblies closest to the camera are destined for passenger 747-400s while the third section along the line is going to be a freighter. Note the upper-deck crew escape door on the cargo version.

American involvement was much higher on the DC-10 than on the TriStar, again, mainly because the Douglas aircraft were fitted with GE or P&W powerplants. Rohr Corporation, at Chula Vista near San Diego, produced the nacelles, while Garrett of Phoenix, Arizona, supplied the APU and environmental systems. A joint effort between Abex of Canada and Dowty of the United Kingdom produced the nose gear, while the main gear was the responsibility of California-based Howmet. Vought Aerospace produced the horizontal stabilizers, and the upper vertical stabilizer and rudder assembly was produced in Italy.

San Diego-based Convair, which had seen its civil-jetliner work dwindle away to nothing with the end of CV-990 program, seized the opportunity to get involved in the DC-10. The General Dynamics-owned company was responsible for the design and construction of the fuselage sections, which were towed up the coast from San Diego Harbor to Long Beach on barges. The huge sections were put on low loaders and traveled at night along roads to the Douglas factory. This relationship lasted well into the days of the DC-10's successor, the MD-11, but with falling orders and sinking production levels, Convair announced in 1994 that it would terminate the contract with McDonnell Douglas by the end of 1995. In January 1996, the once-famous Convair factory, covering 95 acres, was shut down for good and by 1997 had been demolished.

Production of the fuselage barrels was eventually taken in-house at Long Beach, though many alternatives had been considered, including some sites in Texas, or one at Salt Lake City, Utah. The first MD-11 fuselage produced entirely at McDonnell Douglas began taking shape in November 1995 and was completed the following May as the first MD-11F for Saudia Airlines. In common with contemporary Boeing products, the MD-11 was a more international product than its earlier jetliner relatives. Italy's Alenia, Spain's CASA, Brazil's Embraer, Korea's Korean Air, and Japan's Fuji and Kawasaki all played parts in its construction. The composite expertise of Westland's Aerostructures Division, based on the United Kingdom's Isle of Wight, was also brought in to produce the enlarged—but much lighter—tail-engine intake.

Airbus—Uniting Europe

Airbus faced huge challenges to set up the A300B production line. The group was spread all over Europe, with subcontractors around the world, and spoke different languages. All the parts had to be shipped between the different sites before being

A classic cross-sectional view of the 747 showing the strengthened upper and main decks as well as the beefed-up keel area that holds belly cargo. The boxlike structure visible on the lower deck is the unpressurized nose-wheel bay.

▲ The giant wings of the 747, each weighing around 47,500 pounds when completed with leading- and trailing-edge structures, are positioned in assembly jigs and joined together by the huge center wing box. Almost 54,000 U.S. gallons of fuel can be contained inside the completed wing and center fuel tank. The four engine pylons, or struts, are also added at this stage.

▶ The first of the fuselage subassemblies, the overwing (Section 44) barrel, is lowered onto the wing and locked into position around midnight on a typical shift. Leading-edge flaps, spoilers, and ailerons are attached to the wings and the rest of the fuselage is added. The forward subassembly (Sections 41 and 42) and aft units (Sections 46 and 48) are lowered into position and fixed to the Section 44 around 4 A.M. The tailplane and elevators are then added, and the fin and rudder fitted by the early afternoon. Flaps are also attached, and the huge "canoe" fairings are placed over the flap actuators. Then the nose gear and four main gears are attached to the 747 which can then move to the next position on its own wheels for the first time. This particular 747 was the fifth -400 for Air India.

◀ Forward fuselages, horizontal stabilizers, fins, and rudders lay around on the 767 production line like parts of a giant model airplane. The fin, rudder, and elevator are made in Italy by Alenia, while the horizontal tail is made in Texas by Northrop Grumman. The rear fuselage section to the left of the picture is made by Canadair.

The cavernous side cargo door distinguishes this partly-built 767 as a -300F destined for express-freight specialist United Parcel Service (UPS).

Farther down the line a 767-300 comes together in final body join. The vertical fin has yet to be attached.

delivered to the final assembly line in Toulouse in southern France. All the bits had to fit precisely and had to be delivered exactly on time and in the right order.

The creation of an A310 wing gives one example of the complexities involved. The journey began in Davenport, Iowa, in the American heartland, where the huge ingots of aluminum alloy were rolled and stretched. The basic blocks that would become skins were then shipped to England and taken by road to Chester, near Liverpool. The skins were then machined and formed into wing boxes before going back on the road to Manchester Airport. The wings were flown to Bremen in northern Germany, where they were completed with wing leading-edge slats and Kruger flaps from Belairbus of Belgium, flap tracks and wing tips from Fokker of the Netherlands, and inboard spoilers from Aerospatiale of France. Daimler-Benz Aerospace Airbus (DASA) also added its own flaps and outboard spoilers before sending the wings by air to Toulouse. There, the wings finally met up with the fuselage and were no sooner attached than were back in the air, on their way to Germany again. This time the aircraft landed at Hamburg, where the A310s were completed with interiors and paint schemes.

The vital key to the Airbus assembly process was an air transport large enough to shuttle the huge parts between the widespread Airbus factories that were at the center of the Airbus concept. Airbus found just such an aircraft in the bloated shape of the Super Guppy. The first of these bizarrely enlarged aircraft was originally created by California-based Aero Spacelines to support the U.S. space program. These aircraft were heavily modified Boeing 377s, either from the original Stratocruiser or KC-97 tanker, enormously expanded to look more like ungainly balloons or blimps than like a jetliner. The first Guppys were used to transport parts of Saturn rockets to NASA's launch pads in Florida for the Apollo program.

Aero Spacelines realized the limited, but lucrative, market for so-called outsize cargo jets and developed an even larger version, the Commercial Super Guppy 201. Ironically, it was developed for two U.S. wide-body programs, the DC-10 and TriStar, and was put into service carrying the first few fuselage sections from Convair to Douglas and wings from Avco in Nashville to Palmdale for the TriStar.

The Super Guppy, named after a type of fish found in the Caribbean, was powered by 4,912-shaft-horsepower Allison 501-D22C turboprops in place of the original 2,200-horsepower Wright R-3350-23 radial piston engines used on the B-29 Superfortress and its 377 successor. The circular fuselage was roughly 25 feet, 6 inches across for more than 30 feet of its length. This was more than adequate for the largest Airbus loads at the time, which were the A300 wing set measuring almost 90 feet in length or the fuselage sections measuring around 20 feet in diameter with packing. Loads were put into the Guppy through the aircraft's nose, which was opened by swinging the entire front end of the aircraft out of the way. A small powered wheel was lowered to the ground specially for this purpose and pushed the entire nose assembly to the left through 110 degrees.

Airbus acquired the original 201s from Aero Spacelines, which was later sold to Tracor Aviation. First one, then two

A 767-300 destined for KLM of the Netherlands reaches the end of the production line. Immediately behind it is a 767-300F for UPS with its large side-loading cargo door hinged open. The UPS aircraft has yet to have its engines attached, and large weights have been suspended from the pylons to simulate their mass. Rudders are painted before the rest of the aircraft because they have to be delicately balanced and even the weight of paint can make a difference. In all, it takes up to 300 gallons of paint weighing 1,200 pounds to cover an aircraft the size of a 747.

Super Guppys were soon busy shuttling parts between the United Kingdom, Germany, France, and Spain. Wings from the United Kingdom would be flown to Bremen and then down to Toulouse, or straight from British Aerospace's Filton site in Bristol to France in the case of the A320 and larger A330 and A340 wings. Wing final assembly was then concentrated at Chester where the runway was lengthened to allow the later Airbus-built outsize-cargo plane, the Beluga (see description below), to operate in and out direct. Fuselages from DASA and other parts traveled from Hamburg to Toulouse while others flew to the Airbus factory via Aerospatiale's Saint Nazaire and Nantes sites. Aerospatiale made forward fuselage and nose sections for the A300 and A310 and the nose and center fuselage of the A330 and A340. The Guppys also flew CASA-built tail sections and doors in from Madrid, Spain.

The Boeing-built 777 nose and forward fuselage is mated with center and aft fuselage barrel sections that have been shipped over from Japan. Here night-shift workers watch the historic moment as the Sections 41 and 42 of the first 777 are moved toward final body join. *Boeing*

▲ DC-10 production was ramping up rapidly in the early 1970s to meet the demands, mainly from the U.S. trunk carriers, for the new tri-jet. "Ship 10" for United, pictured nearest the camera, was one of 48 delivered in 1972, the busiest year for the DC-10-10 line. In all, a total of 122 DC-10-10s plus a further nine Series 10CF passenger/freighter convertible aircraft were built before production ended in 1982. *McDonnell Douglas*

▲ Although Building 80 at Long Beach had happily accommodated DC-8 production, the 50-foot truss height proved somewhat of a handicap for the DC-10, which moved down the line without its vertical tail. These were put on after the aircraft exited the "bird farm." The aircraft nearest the camera, although designated as a Series 20, was later renamed the Series 40 after discussions with Northwest Airlines, which was the only customer for it at the time. *McDonnell Douglas*

◄ A busy day on the pre-delivery ramp at Everett. Three distinctive aircraft on the line include the two 747s at the top. The aircraft farthest from the camera is a -400F, which is the last version of the 747 to retain the original upper-deck hump. The 747 beside it is a -400D short-haul domestic shuttle aircraft for ANA and is the only version of the -400 without winglets. The 767 in green primer is a rarely seen new -200 airframe. This aircraft was destined to be the first Airborne Warning and Control System (AWACS) for Japan and by 1996 sported a radar antenna on the fuselage roof and was in flight test.

By the late 1970s the growing workload began to overtake the two aircraft, which were operated for Airbus by Aeromaritime, a charter subsidiary of the French airline UTA. Two more 201 conversions were performed at UTA's engineering site at Le Bourget, near Paris, using the drawings and production rights that Airbus had secured from the then-defunct Aero Spacelines. By the mid-1980s a fleet of four Super Guppys was constantly in motion around the Airbus circuit.

The increasing age of the Super Guppys and the growing size of the Airbus projects, particularly the A330 and A340, forced Airbus to search for a replacement in 1990. Several ideas were proposed, including converting a couple of former-airline A300B4s, but the winning proposal came from DASA and Aerospatiale which suggested the development of a huge transporter based on the much more capable A300-600R. A new consortium called SATIC (Super Airbus Transport International Company) was formed by the two companies to work the program which was formally launched on August 22, 1991, when Airbus's executive committee approved the purchase of four Super Transporters. The $600 million deal included an option on a fifth aircraft.

Sticking with the fish theme, the new aircraft was dubbed the A300-608ST Beluga after an outsized breed of sturgeon. Apart from big increases in lifting capacity and speed, the Beluga tackled some basic problems that had cropped up with the faithful old Super Guppys. One of these had to do with the way the Guppy's nose needed to be swung out of the way to load the cargo. This meant having to disconnect all the flight controls, hydraulics and electrical connections, which took time and required readjustment before flight. The Beluga was therefore designed with a lowered underfloor cockpit that allowed an upward-opening cargo door. This "ant-eater" configuration not only saved around 45 minutes turnaround time on every cargo operation, but it also allowed loading and unloading in winds up to 40 knots. This had been another limitation of the old Guppy, particularly in the bad winter weather of northern Europe.

The first Beluga built from an A300-600R airframe was taken from the production line in Toulouse when it had reached the wing-central fuselage mating point. The unfinished airframe went to an integration site at Colomiers, which is part of the Airbus/Aerospatiale facilities on the same airfield. There, the DASA-built rear fuselage section and Aerospatiale nose sections were added, and the major job of making the bulbous upper fuselage began. The floor was also strengthened at this stage to enable it to carry a maximum payload of more than 105,000 pounds. The larger fin of the A340, plus a 4-foot plug and a dorsal fin, were then added along with auxiliary fins on the horizontal stabilizer to improve lateral stability.

The first Beluga made its five-hour, 21-minute maiden flight on September 13, 1994, and was certified by the French DGAC 13 months later. The first Super Guppy was replaced in late 1995, and all were expected to be retired, on a one-for-one basis, by 1998.

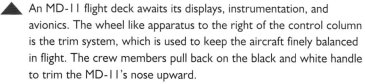 An MD-11 flight deck awaits its displays, instrumentation, and avionics. The wheel like apparatus to the right of the control column is the trim system, which is used to keep the aircraft finely balanced in flight. The crew members pull back on the black and white handle to trim the MD-11's nose upward.

The famous weather of southern California has been useful to McDonnell Douglas, which traditionally completed its aircraft in the open. Here, final touches are made to a Delta MD-11 before the aircraft is painted. Note the distinctive bulged tail engine intake which was made wider than the one on the DC-10 to allow more air into the larger engines of the bigger tri-jet. The yellow-labeled box on the side of the engine is an electronic control unit.

The lower deck of the MD-11 under final assembly. It can hold up to 32 LD-3 containers, or freight totaling around 90,000 pounds. On the main deck, the freighter version of the MD-11 holds up to 26 freight pallets for a total weight of around 156,000 pounds, making it very popular with cargo airlines.

▲ Lockheed's last attempt to make the TriStar a success was the -500 version which was developed to compete with the long-range DC-10 Series 30. Although Lockheed forecast sales of almost 250, only a fifth of these were actually made, and the decision was made to close down the line the year after this picture was taken in 1980. The LTU aircraft nearest the camera was handed over in April 1980, some 17 days before the British Airways TriStar behind it. The British aircraft was converted into a tanker for the RAF six years later. *Lockheed Martin*

▶ The inside trimmings, reading lights, and passenger service units are among the last items to be fitted to the interior of the MD-11 cabin before final hand-over to the customer, in this case Delta.

The finished aircraft had a usable length of 123 feet, 8 inches and could carry entire fuselages, including large parts of even the A330 and A340. The aircraft's optimum payload of 98,000 pounds was nearly double that of the Super Guppy. Range capability was higher by more than 1,500 nautical miles, and the cruise speed increased to Mach 0.70. The ungainly aircraft could also operate at altitudes up to 37,000 feet, though only the flight deck was pressurized.

Russian Wide-Body Builder

Unlike in the West, where aircraft designer and manufacturer are generally one and the same, the Russian organization was vastly different with separate design bureaus, known as OKBs, and state-run air-craft and engine factories. The OKBs designed aircraft to meet specifications issued by the government, and the winning proposal was handed over to a factory to be built if tests on prototypes were successful. This setup was a product of the centralized structure of the communist Soviet Union and was inherited by the aerospace industry of the Commonwealth of Independent States (CIS) when the Congress of People's Deputies dissolved the Soviet Union in December 1991.

The Ilyushin OKB was one of the oldest Soviet bureaus and was named after its former head of design, Sergei Vladimirovich Ilyushin, who had been developing aircraft since the 1930s.

Lockheed's former "Star Factory in the Desert" is now the Lockheed Martin Skunk Works, home to some of the most advanced and classified military aircraft projects in the United States. Evidence is visible to the sharp eyed who may be able to pick out an F-117A Nighthawk, better known as the Stealth Fighter, nestled between two buildings at bottom right. Above and to the right are two other famous Skunk Works products, the SR-71 Blackbird and U-2 spy plane.

Ilyushin's civil Il-14 and turboprop Il-18, and later the long-range Il-62, made it the preeminent supplier of high-capacity aircraft to Aeroflot, the state-run airline. When Ilyushin beat the other OKBs with its first wide-body design for an "airbus" for Aeroflot, two prototypes were built in 1974 at Moscow's Khodinka Airport at the bureau's headquarters. When the Il-86 was approved, the order was given to the GAZ 40 production plant at Voronezh, around 100 miles south of Moscow on the banks of the River Don.

Again, unlike in the West, where manufacturers subcontracted great chunks of production to outside suppliers, much of the basic aircraft was produced on-site almost from raw materials. These arrived, usually by train, from a network of main lines that extended as far south as the great industrial cities of the Donets Basin, southwest to Kharkov, north to Moscow, and east to Samara, or Kuibyshev, as it had been known, where the engines were made. The Kuibyshev Engine OKB was originally called the

Kuznetsov OKB when the engines for the Il-86 were selected. Named after the general designer Nikolai Dimitrievich Kuznetsov, the bureau had quickly built up a powerful reputation by producing the world's biggest turboprop engine, the 14,700-shaft-horsepower NK-12, for the Soviet Tupolev Tu-95 Bear strategic bomber. Much of its strength was built on a work force of German engineers that had been brought to Russia at the end of World War II. The engine selected for the Il-86 was the NK-86, which had been developed from a series of other turbofans used on the Il-62, Tu-154, and even the supersonic Tu-144.

Production of the Il-86 ceased in 1993 and Vorenezh switched to manufacturing the longer-range Il-96-300 derivative. This was initially powered by the relatively modern high-bypass PS-90 engine, which was shipped by rail to the factory from Perm, several hundred miles to the northwest in the shadow of the Ural Mountains. The first stretched Il-96M was made from the rebuilt Il-96-300 prototype and powered by P&W PW2337 turbofans. These were shipped to Russia along with avionics from the U.S. manufacturer Rockwell Collins. Although the program got off to a slow start because of funding shortages, the prospects of a full-scale go-ahead led to plans for the Voronezh factory to be upgraded to support higher production rates than the six per year of the Il-96-300. By the mid-1990s Ilyushin had shaped plans to make at least 225 Il-96Ms, compared to a total of 104 Il-86s produced between 1976 (when serial production began) and 1993.

▲ The bulbous Super Guppy noses its way into Manchester International Airport on a sullen July day in 1996. The Guppy's first job was to carry parts of Saturn rockets for the Apollo program.

▼ The last-ever Airbus wing sets to be flown from Manchester by Guppy are loaded later the same morning. These particular wings will eventually be attached to an A319 in Hamburg, Germany, for Swissair.

A huge multi-purpose A330/340 wing is prepared for shipment by British Aerospace to Toulouse. The concept of a common wing is described by Airbus vice-president for strategic planning, Adam Brown, as "a piece of brilliant insight." Until the advent of the A3XX, the structure was the biggest production wing ever built in Britain or anywhere else in Western Europe. *British Aerospace Airbus Chester*

An A310-300 bound for Delta moves down the original Airbus production line in Toulouse in 1993. The relatively tight squeeze meant that new facilities were needed for the larger A330/340 family. *Airbus Industrie*

The Beluga can fly at speeds up to Mach 0.7 (484 miles per hour) and has a range of 1,035 miles with a maximum payload of more than 100,000 pounds, or roughly double that of the Super Guppy. It can cruise at altitudes up to 37,000 feet. This aircraft flew for the first time on September 13, 1994. *Airbus Industrie*

The old and the new. The first two Belugas sit in the sunshine beside the last two Super Guppys by the new Clement Ader A330/340 final-assembly site at Toulouse. The advanced transporters have a turnaround time of less than 45 minutes compared to several hours for the old Super Guppys. *Airbus Industrie*

The second of four A300-600ST Belugas demonstrates its huge capacity for giant jetliner parts as it disgorges a rear fuselage section. The $1 billion Beluga development program was handled by SATIC, a joint venture of Aerospatiale and Diamler-Benz Aerospace Airbus. The height of the loading door, when open, is 55 feet, exposing a cylinder with a usable length of more than 123 feet and a width of 70 feet. *Airbus Industrie*

The huge six-wheel main gear truck and enormous GE90 engine loom large in this close-up of a British Airways 777-200 on finals to London Heathrow. This was the first production 777 delivered to British Airways and is named *Sir Charles Edward Kingsford Smith* after the pioneer who flew the first trans-Pacific flight in *Southern Cross*, a Fokker F.VII monoplane, from San Francisco to Brisbane, Australia, via Honolulu and Suva in 1928.

Eastern helped launch the TriStar with an order for 50 in 1968. One of its fleet is captured touching down at Miami 20 years later not long before the airline collapsed.

FIELD OF DREAMS—THE OPERATOR'S ROLE

5

IT HAS BEEN A WELL-KNOWN JOKE IN THE INDUSTRY THAT the airlines are the last to be asked about the design of a new airliner. They are, after all, merely the operators! Some referred to it as the "Field of Dreams" philosophy, after the movie in which a baseball stadium was built in the middle of nowhere in the belief that "if you build it they will come." In the aviation world this was translated simply into: "If you build it they will buy it."

This rather one-dimensional attitude showed the first significant signs of change in the mid-1980s as Airbus, Boeing, and McDonnell Douglas all sought more and more customer feedback on the development of the A330, A340, 747-400, and MD-11. For the first time manufacturers actually began asking airlines what they thought of their design ideas before they were committed to go ahead. "It was the realization," said a Boeing engineer, "that we knew how to build airplanes but we didn't know anything about how to operate them!"

Boeing took customer involvement to an all-time high with the design and development of the 777. This was a twin-jet design originally conceived in 1986 as a transcontinental replacement for the DC-10 and TriStar. Boeing planned to keep it simple by using the 767 as a foundation for the new jet, which was consequently called the 767-X. Boeing's problem was that it was catching up with Airbus and McDonnell Douglas, both of which had already begun work on new aircraft with similar capacity. So the Seattle company decided that the only way to produce the right jetliner for the market was to ask the market what it wanted. This may seem obvious in hindsight, but it was a very unusual move at the time. Airlines had traditionally issued requirements and specifications but had rarely provided the sort of detailed input Boeing was looking for.

Boeing's "market-driven" initiative was to give it some big surprises. For a start, none of the airlines really wanted a derivative based on the 767. Boeing had juggled with the basic 767 design to increase capacity by stretching it and adding winglets. At one stage it even grafted part of a 757 fuselage onto the back of the 767 to provide a one-and-a-half double decker. The airlines quickly rejected "the Hunchback of Mukilteo," as the ugly hybrid was dubbed after a local area, along with other 767-based options. Most wanted a wider cabin cross-section, and Cathay Pacific of Hong Kong pushed Boeing for a cabin width of 747-like proportions.

United became the focus for the Boeing 767-X program when it announced it was looking for a long-term replacement for its fleet of DC-10s, or Diesel 10s as they were nicknamed by the carrier. With market prospects looking good, the Boeing board gave the go-ahead in December 1989 to start issuing firm offers to airlines on the 767-X. The following month Boeing invited a group of major airlines to come to Seattle and establish the basic configuration. This first "Working Together" group included heavyweights such as ANA, American Airlines, British Airways, Cathay Pacific Airways, Delta Air Lines, Japan Airlines, Qantas Airways, and of course, United. Each airline was asked to fill out a 23-page questionnaire about what it wanted to see on the new aircraft.

By March 1990 the "Working Together" group had produced the basic configuration of an aircraft much bigger and bolder in concept than Boeing's original idea. It was to carry 325 passengers in three classes and have 10 percent better seat-mile costs

Boeing's first perfectly circular jetliner was the 777. Cathay Pacific was one of the airlines that influenced the decision to make the 777 almost as wide as the 747.

▼ British Airways generated more than 100 changes to the baseline 777 including radial-ply ties, an on-board engine-vibration monitoring system, and a revised aft galley. Here, one of the first GE90-powered test aircraft, later registered G-ZZZB, lands on Runway 34L at Boeing Field after the end of yet another sortie.

than the A330 or MD-11. It would also have the very latest fly-by-wire flight-control technology and a sophisticated "glass" cockpit based on the 747-400, but with a 767-style systems architecture. The interior configuration would be made totally flexible, so airlines could quickly adapt to different market conditions by changing the capacity of different seating classes, such as increasing business seating and reducing first and economy, or vice-versa.

In October 1990, United conducted a grueling two-day marathon session with all the airframe and enginemakers to thrash out the final selection for its DC-10 replacement effort. Finally, on the afternoon of Saturday, October 14, United announced it had signed a letter of intent for 34 P&W-powered 777s, which the 767-X had now become. The next month, a development team from United moved into Boeing's offices. Until then, customer engineers had occupied Portakabins by the flight line or small offices in an area of the delivery center called "airline row" which was far away from any design work in Everett or

◄ Some of the design improvements on the 777 were modest but just as important to the airlines as any of the much larger technical breakthroughs. One such development was the design of the main cabin doors which could easily be swung open or shut by a cabin attendant using only one hand.

▼ The airline ANA influenced the length of the basic 777-200 version by requesting a slightly longer aircraft. The size of the aircraft next to the 767 is apparent in this view of the ramp at Haneda Airport in Japan. Note the JAS A300B in the background, which has a livery based on the early Airbus demonstrator colors.

▲ A Cathay Pacific 777-200 approaches Hong Kong. Cathay is due to operate the first stretched 777-300 beginning in May 1998.

Renton. This time the team from United was soon joined by others from British Airways, ANA, and Japan Airlines in the very heart of the Boeing design effort.

"Working Together" was a new concept and it took time for everyone to adjust to it. In the past, relationships between company engineers and customers ranged from suspicious at best to confrontational at worst. This time they were all expected to get along together and be open about everything with no holds barred! Boeing president and chief executive officer Philip Condit, who was named as the first general manager of the New Airplane Division overseeing the development, said, "Inviting our customers to be genuine partners in the design process was not without its risks. After all, when you let your customers see the inner workings of your company, you risk exposing your shortcomings. Maybe they'll find out you're not as smart and efficient as you say you are. The irony is, however, that the tendency to exclude customers for fear of risking embarrassment can result in delivering a

product that fails to fully meet their needs. And that is the most serious embarrassment of all—one that can rather quickly put you out of business."

In the end, the results were spectacular, although the process was at times frustrating for both sides. Boeing estimated that out of about 1,500 design issues dealt with by the teams, some 300 were new design directions that Boeing would not otherwise have taken. In all, customer insight was reflected in more than 1,000 design modifications to the 777.

Condit said, "Customers didn't tell us how to design a wing or configure the landing gear—but their knowledge was invaluable on items that affect the day-to-day satisfaction of operating the aircraft." Changes were generally tiny but nonetheless significant. "An airline member of one team that was designing an electronics bay pointed out that the light was positioned directly overhead," Condit said. "That seemed a logical place for a light to our engineers. But the airline rep explained that when a maintenance person is actually working in the bay, his head and shoulders block most of the light, making it very difficult to see. He would end up trying to pull out boxes with a flashlight gripped in his teeth. So we changed the design and put two lights on the sides of the bay."

The prototype 777 flies high over the mountains of Washington State during the rigorous test effort, which began on June 12, 1994, and eventually involved nine aircraft and three engine types. *Boeing*

American Airlines suggested a new design of passenger reading light that could be replaced by the crew. The airline had just had to refund a first-class passenger the price of his trans-Pacific ticket from Japan after a failed light over his seat had prevented the passenger from being able to work as he had planned. In response, Boeing developed a design that allowed cabin crew to change a bulb in flight. British Airways produced more than 100 changes to the basic aircraft. These included the adoption of radial-ply tires for the nose gear, making the 777 the first U.S. commercial jet to be certified with radial-ply tires as standard equipment. Others included a maintenance-friendly on-board engine-vibration system and a revised aft galley design that provided room for four extra seats.

United suggested significant changes, including a revised trailing-flap design that could be disassembled into two parts so that it could fit into an autoclave for repair. Boeing originally planned to make the 43-foot-long composite structure in one piece. United also pushed for redesigned parts that would make the aircraft easy to maintain. These included the replacement of one long leading-edge access panel with several smaller ones so the mechanic would not need to remove scores of screws to find one problem. Contributions from other airlines included a new wing fueling point accessible with standard equipment and even a "no-slam-can" lavatory-seat design that would not wake up sleeping passengers!

Even the aircraft's huge, 200-foot-span wing was designed with a fold line 22 feet in from the wing tip, thanks to input from American, which was concerned that the new jet would not fit into gates designed for the smaller-span DC-10. Boeing agreed to the wing-fold option to maintain a large enough wingspan for all future roles. These roles quickly grew from the basic DC-10 and TriStar replacement to include a whole new family of jetliners aimed at everything from ultra-long-haul medium-capacity routes to even a replacement for its own early 747s.

Following the lead set on the 777 design effort, Boeing enrolled potential customers into the early planning stages for its next wide-body venture, the 747-500X and -600X. Airbus took a similar tack with both its A340 stretch studies and the double-decker A3XX plans.

While Eastern and TWA opted for the TriStar, American and United put their weight behind the DC-10. American's original requirement for an "airbus" resulted in both the TriStar and the DC-10. American preferred the Douglas option and launched the world's second giant jetliner with an order for 50 in February 1968. The aircraft pictured taxiing for takeoff at San Juan was delivered to the airline in 1979.

Alitalia was one of the European airlines that gathered to discuss the concept of an "airbus" to counter growing congestion. The result was the A300B which Alitalia duly bought. One of its A300Bs is pictured taxiing behind a company McDonnell Douglas MD-82 in the congested Europe of 1996.

McDonnell Douglas also recruited a large airline advisory board to help with deliberations over the proposed MD-XX tri-jet family, which despite attracting significant interest, was canceled for cost reasons.

Early Influences

The combined influence of airlines on early wide-body history was demonstrated by the group of European airlines that met at the Paris air show in 1965 to discuss their joint requirements for the future (see Chapter 2). Air France, Alitalia, BEA (later part of British Airways), Lufthansa, Sabena, and SAS all forecast booming growth for their short- to medium-haul routes and needed a type of "airbus" seating around 175. European aircraft makers had begun to look at newer high-capacity designs and the meeting provided a much-needed focus for these studies. Therefore, the second meeting, which took place in October 1965, suddenly took on more importance. The original six were now joined by Aer Lingus, Finnair, KLM, Swissair, and TAP (of Portugal), along with industry and government representatives. What had begun as an informal get-together to discuss future needs snowballed into a Europe-wide effort that culminated in the creation of Airbus Industrie in 1970.

The proposed "airbus" gradually grew in size until it was almost double the size of the original specification. However, the Airbus partners later decided to scale the A300, as it became known, back down to around 250 seats after potential European operators such as Air France and Lufthansa showed concern that it had been getting too big. Successive members of the Airbus

family incorporated more new technology, which became a hallmark of the European company. Airbus led the way in developing advanced "glass-cockpit" flight decks with CRT types of instrument displays and integrated systems that eliminated the need for a flight engineer. Such developments as the Forward Facing Crew Cockpit required intensive cooperation with airlines, which became more closely involved than ever before.

Some airline design influences have ended up becoming far more important to the long-term future of the aircraft than even the manufacturer had originally thought. The 747's upper-deck hump, for example, was created because both Pan Am and Boeing believed most of them would eventually be converted to nose-loaded cargo carriers after the main passenger routes had been taken over by SSTs. The upper deck, originally intended as a crew rest area, later took on a life of its own as a passenger area. The capacity of the upper deck grew with each version until achieving a maximum capacity of around 100 in the late 1990s.

The 767 is another wide-body that profited from changes demanded by a customer. The twin-jet ended up with bigger wings than expected because United wanted it to be able to climb straight to 40,000 feet and operate a full load from Denver's high-altitude airport. The extra-large wing allowed Boeing to develop the extended-range 767-200 and, even more important, made the 767-300 stretch a relatively easy task. The -300 and -300ERs subsequently proved to be more popular than the shorter versions, extending the life of the program by more than two decades and providing the basis of the 767-400 which was launched in March 1997.

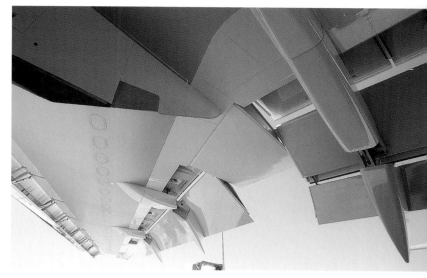

▲ The big wing of a Qantas 767-300ER is pictured fresh out of the Everett factory in Washington. The wing of the long-range -300 contains 24,100 U.S. gallons and, with a small tip extension, provided the basis for the even longer 767-400 launched by Boeing in early 1997.

▼ One of its biggest effects of the United input into the 767 was the larger wing which allowed the aircraft to operate comfortably out of the high-altitude airport at Denver. In later life this big wing enabled Boeing to easily stretch the 767 and gave it ample fuel capacity for long-range over-water flights. The 767 later came to dominate the North Atlantic. This ETOPS-capable aircraft is appropriately called *City of Denver*.

This strange looking Il-86 was first seen at the once top-secret Russian flight research center at Zhukovsky in 1992. Although it superficially resembles the Boeing 767 AST, it is in fact more closely akin to the USAF E-4B airborne command post. The canoe-shaped housing on the roof contains a satellite communications antenna. The aircraft is designated by Ilyushin as the Il-80 and is code-named Maxdome by NATO.

This ungainly looking aircraft began life as the 767 prototype but was later converted into the Airborne Optical Adjunct for use in the Star Wars effort. The big, boat-shaped cupola on the fuselage roof houses infrared tracking devices that reportedly can detect the heat of a human body against the cold background of space at a range of 1,000 miles! Although the SDI, or Star Wars, program was dropped, the 767 is now employed in a similar role for the Ballistic Missile Defense Organization which calls it the Airborne Surveillance Testbed (AST). The telescopes now hunt for the hot flare of a ballistic missile being launched and pass on the data to other aircraft armed with lasers which would then destroy the missile.

Technical Sergeant Don Cox eases the boom of the KC-10A down toward a thirsty McDonnell Douglas F-4E of the 334th Tactical Fighter Squadron on one of the last operational sorties for the old fighter en route to an exercise over Puerto Rico. The aerial refueling officer "flies" the boom through a specially developed fly-by-wire control system that controls the boom's elevator and dual rudders.

The USAF's fleet of KC-10A Extenders have served in every recent conflict involving the United States, including the support of Operations Desert Shield and Desert Storm. Fuel load at takeoff can be up to almost 350,000 pounds, and the aircraft can deliver 200,000 pounds of fuel to other aircraft up to 2,200 miles from base. This KC-10A, *Peace Maker,* is poised to land on Runway 26 at Seymour Johnson AFB, North Carolina.

Warplanes and Biz-Jets

It was not only the airlines that profited from the giant leap in capacity offered by the wide-body revolution. The long range and huge payload of the jumbo generation was quickly seized upon by the military, particularly in the United States where military versions of the 747, 767, and DC-10 were soon developed.

The original 767 prototype was converted into a huge flying observation platform for the U.S. Defense Department's Strategic Defense Initiative (SDI). A massive, boat-shaped cupola was built onto the roof of the forward fuselage and stuffed with conventional camera, telescopes, and infrared tracking devices. The 767 would patrol at high altitude, and its visual systems were trained on missiles and targets in the stratosphere. After SDI was canceled, the airborne optical adjunct (AOA), as the ungainly looking twin-jet was called, was converted again into the airborne-surveillance testbed. Although the title had changed, its job was still roughly the same. Careful design had gone into the shape of the cupola so that the air rushing past the "windows" would not cause any optical distortion to the tracking devices. Even though the 767 could only cruise at 0.8 Mach, the air flowing past the curved roof is accelerated up to supersonic speeds.

This design work was to prove useful in late 1996 when a Boeing-led team with Lockheed Martin and TRW won a $1.1 billion contract to produce a prototype attack-laser aircraft for the USAF. The YAL-1A was actually based on the 747-400F and was designed to use a nose-mounted chemical laser to hit ballistic missiles in mid-air. The

▲ A USAF Boeing E-4B National Emergency Airborne Command Post "somewhere" in Texas. The main operating base for the four-strong fleet is Offut AFB, Nebraska. The second hump on the spine of the aircraft, which has a normal crew of up to 94, encloses a super-high-frequency (SHF) satellite communications dish. The E-4B can also trail a five-mile-long wire in its wake that acts as a very-low-frequency antenna.

▲ The sole 747-300 operated as a state transport is owned by the Saudi Arabian government. The aircraft sports a large satellite antenna similar to the E-4B and has a luxurious interior with several state, conference, and private bedrooms. The irregular windows give some clue as to the unusual interior.

early AOA design helped Boeing because it gave the company the know-how and confidence to develop a nose-mounted laser turret that would not be badly affected by airflow distortion.

The AL-1A (as the production version of the airborne-laser 747 would be called) was developed to combat the threat of "theater" missiles such as the Scud used by Iraq during the Gulf War. The laser was designed to fire up to 30 times, for five seconds a shot, at targets up to 360 nautical miles away. Each shot of the oxygen-iodine laser was expected to cost around $1,000 and would be aimed at the missile during the first 80 to 140 seconds of flight during what was called the boost phase.

If the tests proved successful, the USAF planned to operate a fleet of seven laser-equipped 747s by 2006. Some were to remain in the United States at all times to defend the home country from surprise missile attack while others could be deployed to hot spots around the world in time of conflict.

The airborne-laser 747 was joining an established USAF force of other military 747 versions. Two were designated VC-25As and performed the role of *Air Force One*, the U.S. presidential transport. The heavily modified 747-200Bs, powered by GE engines, replaced the elderly VC-137 versions of the 707. They were fitted with special communications systems and self-protection such as chaff and flares to decoy infrared guided missiles. The VC-25As were also fitted with electronic jamming countermeasures to protect them against more sophisticated missiles. Inside, they were luxuriously appointed with state rooms, staff areas, sleeping accommodations, and washroom facilities. Private cabins for the president and first lady were built into the nose area.

Because the 747 offered almost three times the payload of the 707, the USAF also replaced the EC-135 (military 707 version) with the 747-based E-4 as its main airborne-command-post aircraft. These were designed to provide the critical link between the U.S. National Command Authority (NCA) and the nation's strategic retaliatory forces during and following a conventional or

nuclear attack on the United States. Four E-4s were delivered in the 1970s and were later upgraded to E-4B standard.

In its E-4B guise, the 747 has a much bigger air-conditioning capability (up to a minimum of 8,000 cubic feet per minute) to cool the huge amount of avionics aboard. It is also shielded against the electro-magnetic pulse effects of an exploding nuclear bomb that would otherwise damage or destroy all the avionics aboard. To help with communications with submarines and other missile forces, a long wire antenna is fitted to a drum, from which it could be trailed out into the slipstream from a cone in the tail near the APU. The wire could be trailed out for up to 5 miles behind the E-4B to provide very low frequency/low frequency (VLF/LF) communications, which are very hard to jam. A curious-looking bulge on the roof, resembling a second hump, houses a super high frequency (SHF) satellite link.

The E-4 was also the first true three-decker jumbo; the lower deck is extensively used for crew, and not just baggage. Together with the main and upper deck, the E-4B has room for 94 crew. It also houses an NCA area, conference room, briefing room, battle-staff work area, communications control center, technical control center, crew rest, and maintenance area. The rear lower lobe area also houses a winch operator's station for the VLF/LF antenna. To help in its role during national emergencies, the E-4B is designed to be able to tie into commercial TV and radio networks, so it could be used to broadcast to the population. On the ground, it can also be connected (and quickly disconnected) to a ground communications network.

In the familiar parallel universe that existed between the U.S. military and its counterpart in the former Soviet Union, it was not long before the Russian equivalent of the E-4B was seen. The aircraft turned out to be a military version of the Il-86, which Ilyushin called the Il-80 and to which NATO gave the code name Maxdome. It was first seen at the former top-secret Zhukovsky Flight Research Center in 1992 and, although it superficially resembled the 767 AOA, was instant-

The unique space and range of the 747SP made it into one of the world's biggest private jets. By 1997 at least 12 were operated as business, state, or private transports—more than a quarter of the entire fleet! The SP pictured here was delivered originally to Braniff Airways and later flew with both Pan Am and United before finally passing into the ownership of the government of Oman.

Not to be left behind, even the Russians have taken to using wide-bodies as private aircraft. This Il-96-300 provided Russian premier Boris Yeltsin with transport during the mid-1990s, replacing the obsolete Il-62.

ly recognized as the aircraft that would be used by Russia's commander-in-chief in the event of war.

Although it still carried civil Aeroflot markings, the biggest give-away to its military role was a large boat-shaped fairing above the forward fuselage. Like the E-4B's second hump, this fairing covered a satellite-communications antenna, and an attachment under the lower port side of the fuselage appeared to contain a drogue for a VLF trailing-wire antenna. The aircraft was also hardened against nuclear blast and did not have any passenger-cabin windows. Under the wings are large pods that contained big, turbine-driven electric generators.

Another natural role for the big jets is as an airborne tanker. The Handley Page Victors of the U.K. Royal Air Force (RAF) tanker fleet was badly depleted after the campaign to recapture the Falkland Islands in 1982, and the RAF desperately needed new capacity. In response, it bought six TriStar 500s from British Airways in March 1983 and sent them to Marshall Aerospace of Cambridge, England, for modifications. The TriStars were converted into dual tankers and troop transports.

Extra fuel tanks were fitted into the freight bays in the belly to increase total capacity to 100,000 pounds. Two hose-drum refueling units and a closed-circuit TV system were installed in the rear fuselage. Three of the TriStars were also fitted with 140-inch by 102-inch side cargo doors. A further three former-Pan Am TriStars were also bought by the RAF, which had them converted into troop transports.

The USAF bought 60 DC-10s to form a fleet of tankers in exactly the same way. The tankers, dubbed KC-10A Extenders, were basically military versions of the DC-10-30CF (convertible freighter), painted green, with the windows deleted. The aircraft were also fitted with an in-flight refueling receptacle above the cockpit so that they could receive fuel in-flight from other tankers. A single refueling boom was installed under the aft fuselage for refueling USAF aircraft while hose-and-drogues were fitted to the wings to refuel U.S. Marine Corps and U.S. Navy aircraft. The Royal Netherlands Air Force also decided to convert two former-KLM DC-10s into tankers, which were dubbed KDC-10s.

▲ One of the most luxuriously equipped A340-200s ever built, this early production aircraft served briefly with Lufthansa in 1993 before swapping passengers for members of the Brunei royal family.

Giant jetliners also provide the ultimate in biz-jets. The majority of the world's largest biz-jets, most of them being the larger members of the Airbus family, or versions of the 747, usually the 747-400 or 747SP, are owned by members of royal families from the oil-rich nations of the Middle East. The aircraft are generally extravagantly outfitted with plush state rooms, dining rooms, bedrooms (with gold-plated faucets), built-in spas and bathing facilities, large kitchens, and even servants' quarters. The aircraft are also often equipped with sophisticated communications centers and on-board entertainment facilities such as mini-cinemas.

The Final Frontier

Other wide-bodies have been employed in very special roles. One of the first A300Bs built, for example, was converted to train astronauts for zero-g conditions. The aircraft replaced an old Sud-Aviation Caravelle and was the first wide-body in the world to offer so much room for weightlessness experiences. The program involved Novespace, the French space agency CNES, and Sogerma.

Another space-related, though completely different specialist role for a wide-body, was the use of a TriStar as a satellite launcher. The former Air Canada L-1011 TriStar 100 was converted by Marshall Aerospace for Orbital Sciences Corporation of Fairfax, Virginia, to send its Pegasus air-launched booster into low-earth orbit. The company originally leased a USAF B-52 for launches but selected the TriStar as a replacement in 1992. The aircraft was modified with an attachment system to carry the 40,000-pound-plus winged rocket beneath the belly between the main undercarriage legs. The Pegasus, which was originally designed to carry payloads of up to 1,000 pounds into space, is dropped from the aircraft before deploying its stabilizers and firing the rocket motor.

NASA also employs two 747s to carry the Space Shuttle Orbiter piggyback-style between the landing site at Edwards Air Force Base (AFB), California, and the launch site at Cape Canaveral, Florida. The former American Airlines 747s were modified with a carrying cradle assembly mounted on the top of the fuselage and have never been permitted to fly above Mach 0.6 and 26,000 feet, with or without the Orbiter attached.

Other unique roles for wide-bodies include a DC-10 that was converted for use by Orbis as a flying eye-surgery hospital to tour developing areas of the world where specialist eye care is not normally available. A similar but perhaps more ambitious conversion was undertaken by Lockheed Martin Aircraft Service Company which transformed a former Worldways Canada TriStar 100 into the world's first privately owned hospital aircraft.

The flying hospital, owned by Pat Robertson's Operation Blessing, based in Virginia, was aimed at providing a fully equipped outpatient medical facility for sick people in developing countries. The aircraft was fitted with seating for up to 67 people, a surgery with up to four operating stations, two dental stations and a pre- and post-operation recovery area for up to 12 patients. On-board equipment

▲ Another early-build Airbus, this time an A300, is now being used to provide periods of weightlessness for training astronauts and for preparing micro-gravity equipment and experiments for space missions. This modern "vomit comet" replaced a French-space-agency Caravelle and gives up to 25 seconds of zero-G. It is the first wide-body to be used anywhere in the world for such a purpose.

includes x-ray machines, a fluoroscope, autoclave sterilizers, and other laboratory equipment. The aircraft was designed to service up to 50 surgical patients a day and could carry enough supplies to be in the field for up to 10 days. The aircraft could make up to 12 missions per year with a total time of 19 days required for an average mission, including turnaround time for preparing for the next trip. The Operation Blessing aircraft is truly a hospital and provides a wide range of services, including plastic, orthopedic, and general surgery; major trauma treatment; ophthalmology; and pediatric care.

Patients enter the aircraft through a lower-deck door leading into a reception area and pharmacy. A stairwell provides access to the upper deck which contains the operation rooms, pre-op and post-op recovery area, dental suites, and nurses' station. The TriStar was even equipped with its own purification system with micron filters and bromine cartridges to produce pure water from local sources. It was also supplied with a ground APU and a diesel generator to provide 190 kilowatts of electricity, as well as an on-board oxygen-generating system to produce 90 percent oxygen at a rate of 70 liters per minute. Little could American Airlines have realized in 1965, as it drew up its specification for a new airliner, that it was also providing the blueprint for the ideal flying hospital!

▲ One of the most unusual roles for a wide-body, or for any aircraft, is as a flying hospital. This TriStar, operated by Operation Blessing International, not only provides facilities to treat patients in developing countries, but also has a teaching area for up to 67 people. A closed-circuit television system enables a group to observe an operation and hear the surgeon's voice as the procedure is explained. An ex-Novair DC-10-10 is used in a similar way by the charity Orbis International as a flying eye hospital. The needs for such roving hospitals are real. The World Health Organization recently stated that there are 42 million sightless people in the world, around 70 percent of them needlessly so.

Twenty-five years after the 747 was put through torture it was the turn of the 777. Here one of the wings is pictured being bent and pummeled by more than 100 hydraulic actuators in a fatigue-test rig. The tests continued 24 hours a day to simulate thousands of continuous take-offs, climbs, cruise conditions, descents, and landings, and are designed to expose any serious structural weaknesses before they show up on the real thing in later life. Tests concluded in March 1997 after 120,000 cycles representing 60 years in service

All giant jetliners face the huge challenge of designing exits that are sufficiently wide and numerous to evacuate all passengers in less than 90 seconds in darkness or reduced visibility with only half the exits available.

KEEPING DANGER AT BAY

THE BIGGEST CHALLENGE IN GIANT-JETLINER DESIGN FROM the beginning was safety. How could an airliner carrying upward of 350 passengers close to the speed of sound be designed to be inherently safe and free of defects?

In the early days, when the biggest jetliners of the time were less than half the size of the first wide-bodies then being sketched out, there were even more questions. Would the traveling public dare to travel in such monsters, and—if that were not the case—would the airlines be happy to buy them?

"Here we were designing a 350-passenger airplane, which was huge at the time, and safety was the biggest issue on the designer's mind," said Boeing's Joe Sutter. The company's job, as they saw it, was to ensure reliability and efficiency without affecting the major priority, that of safety. The sheer size of the aircraft would somehow be made to inspire confidence, rather than put people off. "We worked very hard to make sure there was nothing built into the airplane to cause anyone to shy away from it," he added. "Let's say the pilots did not want to fly it, or the passengers did not want to ride in it, or if it had incidents that would cause concern, then I think the whole program would not have been a success. So that was on our minds continually."

Multiple redundancy is the hallmark of safety by design. The more backups available, the less chance of a bad accident. Boeing originally toyed with a three-legged main gear for the 747 but ended up with four, a decision that has since prevented many serious accidents from occurring. The sheer size of the 747's large wings and flaps also created an unexpected "cushion" ground effect that often made for smooth landings. In the words of 747 test pilot Jack Waddell, "It is ridiculously easy to fly; it almost lands itself."

The main result was a design that had more fall-back, or redundant, systems than any aircraft built before it. "A lot of things were placed inside the airplane to give it the ability to survive incidents, such as split control systems, inboard and outboard ailerons, split spoilers, split elevators and split rudders," said Sutter. Redundancy did not stop there. "All those systems were being powered by four hydraulic systems, which was a brand-new innovation," he added. In addition, the big aircraft was designed with a four-legged main landing gear ". . . so that if something happened to part of the landing gear, the pilot could still bring home the airplane successfully," Sutter continued.

Because the 747 was so huge, the forces on the flight controls were far too high to be controlled manually in a standby mode. This was another reason why so many redundancies were built into it. The system was, therefore, designed to cope with a staggering number of possible emergency situations. These included a whole engine dropping off the wing or the loss of an entire outer section of wing, upper section of the tail fin, or even the outboard section of the tailplane and elevator. It was also intended that the aircraft could be controlled when any or all engines failed and could take off with one engine not working.

The rugged nature of the 747 has proved itself time and time again as a result. The second 747-100 built, N747PA, hit the runway lights on takeoff from Runway 01R at San Francisco International in July 1971 and wiped out major parts of the undercarriage, some of which thrust upward through the cabin floor and wedged in the tail. The crew dumped fuel and, thanks to the multiple system redundancy, still made it back for a safe landing on what was left of the landing gear.

In February 1985 a 747SP was cruising over the Pacific at 41,000 feet when the number-four engine apparently failed. The crew called for permission to descend and carry out an air-start. Suddenly, the 747SP slipped out of control and went into a steep spiral dive toward the ocean. The crew fought for control and managed to recover at 11,000 feet, but the three remaining engines had flamed out and had to be restarted as the giant jet dropped below 9,500 feet. The outboard elevators and many other control surfaces were ripped off in the effort to pull out of the dive, as were sections of the flaps. The ends of the stabilizers were actually twisted upward out of shape by the force of pulling out of the dive. Miraculously, the aircraft limped in to San Francisco for a safe landing and was later repaired and eventually put back into service.

At other times, the aircraft and their crews have not been so lucky, despite the built-in redundancy. In separate instances, two

▲ Split rudders on this El Al 747 tail are more evidence of system redundancy.

▼ Not everything went smoothly with early flight tests of the 747. Crews were still getting used to the huge aircraft and the high mounted flight deck. On December 13, 1969, a 747-121 test aircraft destined for Pan Am was being ferried to Renton for refurbishment into airline configuration. Unfortunately, the crew misjudged the approach and touched down 19 feet short and 30 inches below the runway level, ripping the right gear out of its supports. The right wing dropped, and the two right hand engines scraped along the runway, causing considerable damage. The pilot was promptly fired. *Boeing*

▲ All 747 engine pylons and fuse pins were redesigned as a result of a number of incidents and two crashes in which engines came off the wing in flight. Although originally designed to fall clear of the wing, the engine sometimes caused catastrophic damage to the wing and neighboring engine as it fell away. The new design keeps the engine on the wing even after an engine seizure.

freighter versions crashed after an engine came off in flight. The problems were traced to the attachments that held the engines to the pylons, or struts, on the wing. At the heart of the attachments were "fuse" pins that were originally designed to break under extreme stress and let the engine fall off. This was part of a design philosophy stretching back to the days of the piston engine when it was often safer to let a critically damaged engine or propeller fall away from the aircraft than to leave it to cripple the aircraft and cause it to crash.

Until the 747, every Boeing jetliner engine attachment had been designed to break if severe stresses were encountered. Boeing 707s have even been known to survive losing two engines from the same wing and still land safely. One such event happened to a USAF KC-135 tanker (the military version of the 707) during the Gulf War. Both starboard engines of a 707-321C freighter were lost at 36,000 feet over the Swiss Alps in March 1992. With the wing on fire, no flaps, only two engines, and a 25-knot tailwind, the crew managed to land at a French air force base at the high speed of 190 knots.

An MD-11 fitted with a revolutionary power-control system makes the historic first-ever landing of a throttles-only controlled airliner at Edwards AFB, California, on August 29, 1995. Note the NASA F-18 chase aircraft looking on in the background. *NASA*

The wreckage of the wing and engine struts from the 747 freighters was analyzed, which in the case of the first crash, in Taiwan, involved a major search of the bed of the South China Sea. It was confirmed that the fuse pins were the prime suspects in both cases. A new design was developed for all 747s that would keep the engine on the wing at all times except during a crash landing when the engines would break off, so protecting the fuel tanks in the wings.

Engine-related issues also affected the DC-10. In 1979, a DC-10 crashed on takeoff from Chicago O'Hare when a wing-mounted engine broke loose and rotated back over the top of the wing as the aircraft lifted off the runway. The crew might have been able to maintain control but for the damage that the engine caused to the wing's hydraulic system and high lift devices as it broke free. The aircraft lost lift on the damaged side and crashed, killing 271 persons. The aircraft's type certificate was withdrawn for more than a month until all DC-10s were finally allowed back into service in mid-July. The accident report revealed that the engine had been incorrectly lifted onto the strut after undergoing maintenance.

Another engine-related accident that befell a DC-10 some 10 years later led to the development of an advanced standby control system by a NASA-led team. The accident occurred when part of the tail engine in the DC-10 exploded and severed the hydraulic systems at a critical point where all three separate systems were affected. The crew had no control over the aircraft's ailerons, elevators, or rudder. However, they still had engine power available from the two surviving wing engines and by clever manipulation of the throttles managed to bring the crippled jetliner in for a crash landing at Sioux City, Iowa. More than half the people on board, some 184, survived.

NASA joined with McDonnell Douglas, P&W, and Honeywell to develop a system called Propulsion Controlled

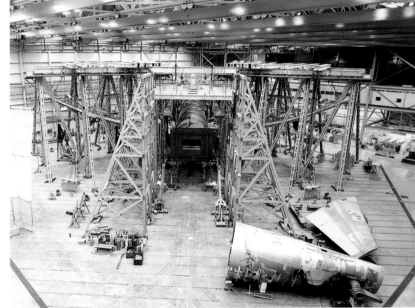

The elastic qualities of the 747 wing were proven during "torture tests" in which the wings were bent up 29 feet before one of them gave way. The dramatic test to destruction proved the wing was capable of taking much higher loads than would be experienced in service. Failure actually occurred at 116 percent of the ultimate design load, or 174 percent of the limit load for the first versions. The failure happened when a simulated load of almost 4g was put on the wing.

Aircraft (PCA), which would enable a crippled jetliner to land safely using engine power alone to control the aircraft. The PCA system was tested first on a modified F-15 Eagle fighter at Edwards AFB, California, where NASA's Dryden Flight Research Center is based. In April 1993, the F-15 made the first landing with the aerodynamic control surfaces locked in place, simulating a total control system failure, and using engine power alone. From here the program concentrated on the main aim, that of testing a PCA on a

Sudden pressure differences between the lower cargo hold and main cabin have caused several incidents and at least one giant jetliner to crash. New floor structures, like the on this 777, use high-strength composite floor beams and have built-in vents to provide instant pressure relief if a hatch, window, or doorway suddenly gives way.

giant jetliner. McDonnell Douglas provided an MD-11 for the attempt, and this jetliner was subsequently used to successfully demonstrate a workable PCA system. The test team discovered that even relatively delicate maneuvers were possible because of the precise engine control that was available through the computerized full authority digital engine control (FADEC) units that are standard fit on virtually all new turbofans. Instead of the flight commands going from the flight deck to the aerodynamic control surfaces, the same pilot commands were interpreted by a separate computer, which translated them into signals for the FADECs. If the pilot wanted to turn to the left, it would tell the right engine's computer to slowly increase power. If the pilot wanted to pitch up and climb, both engines were advanced, and vice versa to descend.

The tests were so successful that all the jetliner manufacturers began inquiring about using PCA as a backup control system for their new wide-body designs. NASA was even considering a further development of its PCA research to investigate a "get-you-home" system for twin-jets. Using similar techniques, the twin PCA would work by controlling the engines in the usual way and by distributing fuel among the wing tanks to change the balance

of the aircraft. NASA hoped it would be possible to develop a system that would be capable of allowing a crippled jetliner to attempt a crash landing with wings level by pumping fuel around the aircraft to keep it balanced.

While flight control and redundancy was one issue, another big worry for all the giant jetliner manufacturers was passenger evacuation. How could so many passengers and crew be expected to evacuate from these huge aircraft within the tight rules? These specified an exit time of 90 seconds using only half the available exits. One of the greatest worries had been getting people down onto the ground from the double-deck level. In the end, all the successful designs were essentially single deck, including the 747, which was not a true double deck in the original design sense. The problem was, therefore, largely avoided by going to a wide-body, single-deck design. Even so, the first versions of the 747 only narrowly met the stiff regulations, which called for, in the case of the first operator Pan Am, the evacuation of all 362 passengers and 19 crew members from five of the eleven emergency doors in 90 seconds flat. In early tests in January 1970, the evacuation target was met but with only three seconds to spare.

The increasing size of jet airliners also led to the development of inflatable slides to help people escape quickly from the aircraft. The pop-open chutes spilled out and inflated to provide a smooth ride to ground level which was now much farther down, particularly from the flight deck and small upper cabin on the 747. The inflatable slides doubled up as life rafts in case of ditching at sea.

Two over-wing exits were designed for the DC-10, when it was suggested that the large area of the wing could be useful as a tem-

Some aircraft have crashed because control runs have been jammed or broken altogether when the floor collapsed because of sudden pressure loss in the cargo hold. Airbus adopted the design philosophy of distributing main and back-up control runs around the circular shell of the fuselage, as well as through the floor beams.

porary "dock" in the event of a successful ditching. This feature was relatively rare at the time but became far more common in later and smaller jetliners. Seat rows on the DC-10 were also staggered so that all passengers sitting by the aisle could get up and move into the aisle at one time. This greatly helped speed up evacuation under normal and emergency situations. In early tests using a special mock-up, 345 passengers and eight cabin staff members managed to escape from the cabin in 76 seconds using only half the exits.

As a result of the focus on swift evacuation, few accidents related to the passengers becoming trapped on board a damaged or burning airliner occurred during the first few decades of widebody operation. Despite the best-laid plans, however, some bad accidents have occurred. One of the worst happened in August 1980 when a Lockheed TriStar 200 carrying pilgrims from Riyadh International Airport to Mecca caught fire shortly after takeoff. Despite smoke in the flight deck and the cabin being engulfed in flames and smoke, the crew managed to land the stricken jetliner back at the airport. Unfortunately all aboard were overcome by smoke and fumes and no one was able to evacuate from the aircraft once it was on the ground.

Pressure and Fatigue

Surprising though it may seem, the huge new jetliners were built almost exactly the same way as their smaller ancestors had been, despite the huge leap in scale. Like many of the generation of jet airliners before them, each was designed with a "fail-safe" structure. This meant that if a part of the airframe should fail or give way for any reason the stresses and loads imposed on that part of the aircraft would be carried by other parts and diverted around the rupture by different "load paths." The new jets were also designed to be fatigue resistant after the lessons learned in the multiple tragedies of the 1950s when two de Havilland Comet jetliners mysteriously crashed within months of each other. The first

Fatigue-test research was performed on an old Japanese short-range 747, which had clocked up thousands of cycles over a relatively short space of time, and on a new 747-400 nose section, to validate design changes made by Boeing to increase the life of the aircraft. The two carcasses now sit forlornly outside the Everett factory in the company of the dismembered parts of other jetliners, including a 777 test airframe.

occurred in January 1954 when a BOAC (the international predecessor of British Airways) Comet crashed into the sea after taking off from Rome, killing all 35 on board. Although flights were suspended for a few weeks, they soon resumed, and almost immediately disaster struck again. A second Comet disappeared over the Mediterranean, killing all 17 passengers and crew members.

In a remarkable feat of salvage for its day, the Royal Navy recovered nearly two-thirds of the sunken plane from very deep water. The wreckage was sent to Farnborough, Hampshire, where it was re-assembled on a frame the size and shape of the Comet. The parts were painstakingly pieced together like a macabre jigsaw puzzle until it suggested that something like an explosion had ripped the airliner apart in midair. No trace of explosives had been found and suspicion fell on the pressurized airframe. In response, another Comet was put into a tank with its wings sticking out. Jacks were put to work bending the wings while water was pumped into the fuselage to re-create the strains equal to those of thousands of hours of flying. Suddenly, the fuselage ripped apart.

▲ Another flight ends safely as this DC-10 nears touchdown.

When the water was drained out it was discovered that cracks had spread from a rivet hole. The cabin had been pressurized, or filled with air at high pressure, to maintain a breathable atmosphere for the passengers since the Comet cruised at high altitudes where people without oxygen masks would normally have gone unconscious. Once the cracks developed, the pressure from the cabin was too much for the structure and it had simply burst open like a balloon.

Most U.S. manufacturers claimed that their designs already took this into consideration even before the lessons of the Comet were fully available, yet the experiences of the ill-fated British jetliner were nevertheless valuable to the whole industry as the first generation of jetliners entered service. From that point on, all jetliners were thoroughly tested for structural defects before entering service. Most manufacturers built two airframes, or major sections of airframes, that never flew but were instead dedicated to tests. One was used for static tests in which the aircraft was basically bent and abused until something gave. The other was used for fatigue tests in which it was pumped up and down to simulate the equivalent of several years in airline service.

The second Boeing 777 airframe, for example, was pulled and stretched until on January 14, 1995, the wings were pulled up 24 feet above their normal position. They snapped at more than one and a half times the load experienced during the most extreme flight conditions. Another airframe, called the fatigue test article, was pressurized to 8.6 pounds per square inch in less than 15 seconds, to simulate the start of a normal flight. Less than 4 minutes later, on average, all the pressure would be released to represent the end of the flight. This was repeated 24 hours a day to build up as many "cycles" (full flights measured from takeoff to landing) as possible before the aircraft is well into production or service. No matter how well designed the jetliner was, something unexpected would quite often show up during testing, and small parts were changed on the production line as a result.

The first 747 fatigue-test airframe was almost totally filled with tiny Styrofoam plastic granules instead of water. It even had small passages inside to let engineers crawl around and inspect certain areas. After 18,000 flight hours had been simulated, some cracks were found in the big keel beam linking the rear and front fuselage sections where the four main undercarriage legs were

continued on page 107

FOLLOWING

▶ Performing Section 41 work on 747s has been steady business for some engineering companies. Here engineers from Hong Kong-based HAECO set about a typical 747 nose section. Note the control cables running back from the cockpit above through the ceiling structure. *HAECO*

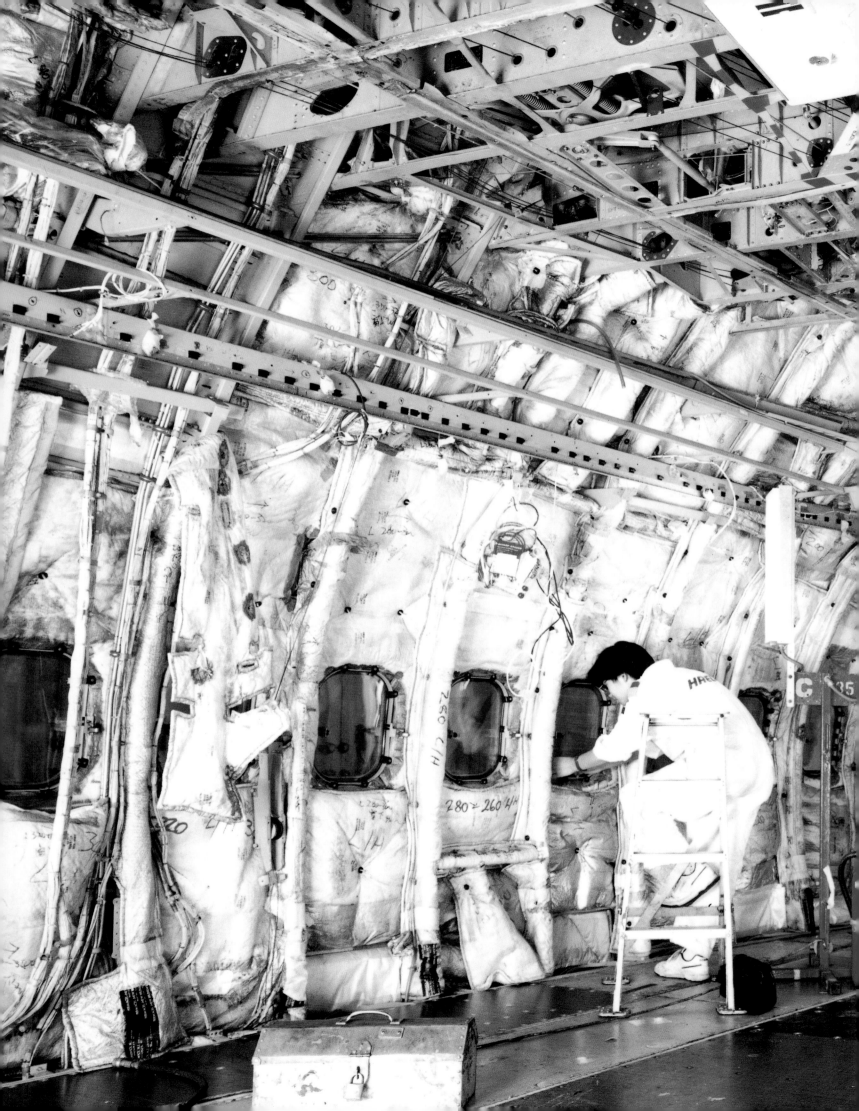

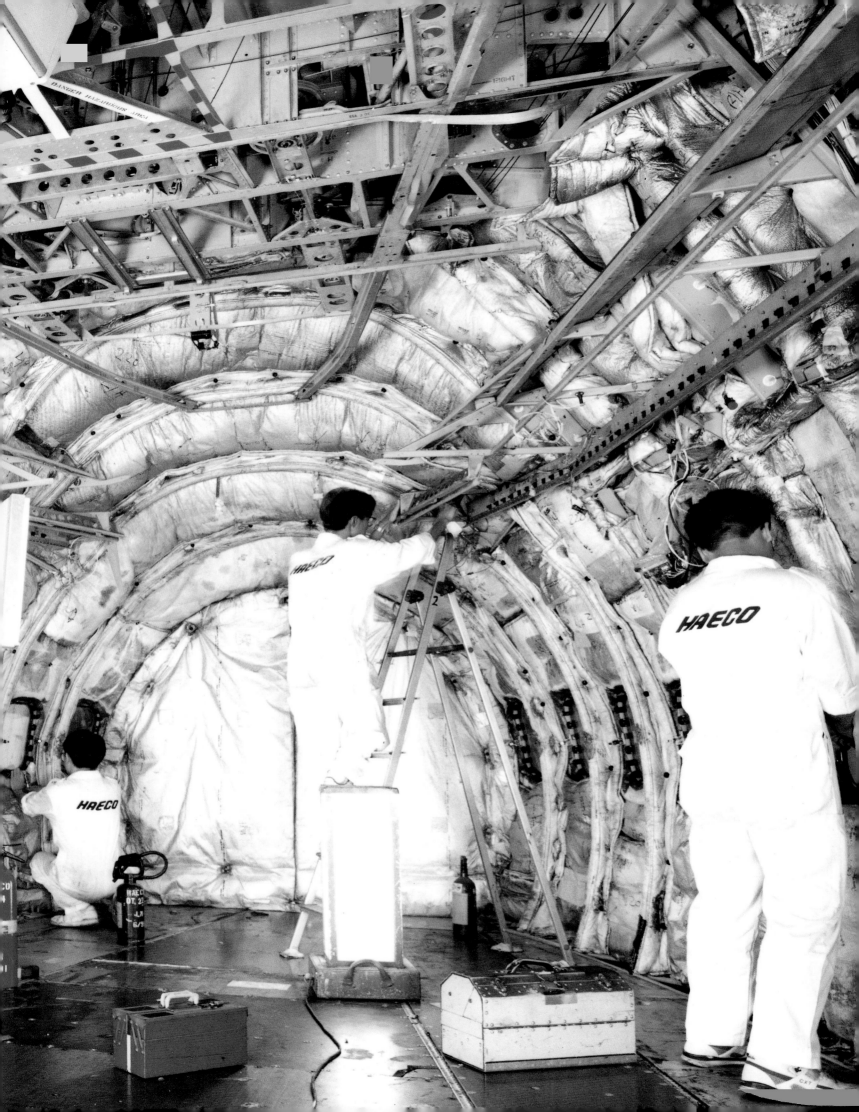

TriStar, and 747 was fitted with them. Each used virtually the same solution which was a series of floor vents at the base of the cabin wall running alongside the seat rails. The vents led to ducts, through which pressurized air would instantly pour to equalize the pressure in the lower holds.

The Airbus design did not require much modification because its power and control runs were widely segregated around the floor, roof, and belly of the fuselage. While main controls ran through the floor in the conventional way, two electrical trim connections ran back to the tail along the inside of the Airbus's roof. Three mechanical trim connections commanding roll, pitch, and yaw also ran through the belly. The distribution of venting, which Airbus had extended as a result of the Paris accident, also meant that the A300B could withstand holes at least 16 square feet in area being blown in either of the two cargo compartments at 38,000 feet altitude without floor damage.

With the alarming increase in terrorism and bomb threats in the late 1970s and early 1980s, a series of new specifications were drawn up by European and U.S. aviation officials. These specifications stipulated that all new wide-body designs must be able to sustain a 20-square-foot hole blown in the side of the fuselage without endangering the floor and essential control runs. One aircraft, the 747-400, was briefly brought under scrutiny by this because only its main deck could meet this criterion; the upper deck was only able to sustain a sudden blowout producing a 12.5-square-foot hole. This became apparent just before delivery of the first 747-400 to KLM, and for some time the delivery schedule was in doubt. Eventually, Boeing agreed to produce a kit to modify the upper deck in return for a temporary operating permit from the European airworthiness authorities. In the revised design, Boeing strengthened the floor and separated out the control runs.

The point about the structural integrity of the 747 was again driven home just three months before the first 747-400 delivery to KLM when, in February 1989, a huge section of fuselage skin ripped away from a United Airlines 747-100 at 22,000 feet over the Pacific. Like the Paris accident 15 years before, the incident was caused by a cargo door opening in flight. This time it was a forward cargo com-

Terrorists have made the 747 a favorite target in the past. In Arizona, this old Evergreen airframe provides a training aid for special U.S. government anti-terrorist forces.

The unusual flat-sided sections around the cockpit of the 747's large nose structure led to some cracking in earlier aircraft.

Continued from page 103

grouped together. Other cracks were found in the rib at the attachment of the wing to the fuselage through which pipes connected the fuel tanks.

It is an unfortunate fact of life that even in our technologically advanced times some lessons have to be learned the most painful way—by accidents. In the early days of wide-body jetliners, for example, it was not realized how disastrous a sudden depressurization could be until a Turkish Airlines DC-10 crashed into a forest near Paris in March 1974, killing all aboard. The aircraft was climbing through 12,000 feet, en route from Paris to London, when a rear cargo door blew open, instantly depressurizing the lower aft section of the jetliner's hold. The cabin floor buckled under the sudden change in pressure and jammed the control cables that ran through the floor to the tail. The aircraft went into a shallow dive and hit the forest 1 minute and 17 seconds after the depressurization at a speed of 420 knots.

This, and an earlier accident involving a partially collapsed rear-cabin floor in a National Airlines DC-10, convinced the industry that vents were needed throughout the cabin in all wide-bodies. The floor vents were made mandatory, and every DC-10,

Boeing had to redesign the upper-deck floor of the 747-400 to meet new regulations covering increased strength and the separation of control runs. The first delivery to KLM was almost delayed as a result.

partment door that opened, causing a cabin depressurization and damage to the number-three and -four engines. Nine people were sucked out and five were injured, but the aircraft survived and made a successful emergency landing in Hawaii with 346 survivors.

Another pressurization failure nearly four years earlier, this time caused by a poor repair of a rear pressure bulkhead, had not ended so well. The aircraft was a Japan Airlines 747-100SR, packed with 520 passengers and crew for a domestic flight. The sudden failure of the rear pressure bulkhead disabled the controls, and the aircraft crashed into Mount Ogura, south of Tokyo. It was the single worst flying disaster in aviation history. The investigation blamed the initial failure on the inadequate repair of the bulkhead which had been damaged in an earlier heavy landing.

The most serious aircraft accident in history, in terms of fatalities, occurred at Tenerife, Canary Islands, in March 1977, when two 747s collided on the runway. One of the aircraft, belonging to KLM, was making its takeoff run in dense fog when the crew members realized that a Pan Am 747 was on the runway ahead of them. The KLM jetliner had already accelerated to almost 145 miles per hour, so its crew decided to attempt to hop its aircraft over the U.S. aircraft. Unfortunately, the left main gear of the KLM 747 hit the top of the Pan Am aircraft just aft of the upper deck. The Dutch aircraft crashed and exploded, killing all aboard, but 61 persons survived on the Pan Am 747. A total of 583 were killed, including those who died later from burns.

Despite this and other tragedies, the overall safety record proved much better, in fact, than first predicted. When the 747 was first rolled out, insurance underwriters predicted that there

would be three fatal 747 crashes in the first 18 months of service. As it turned out, there were actually only five in the first decade, of which three were the result of pilot error.

The unusual bulb-shaped nose of the 747 created other problems for Boeing, particularly in the early models. Some of these were not entirely unexpected. Boeing deliberately beefed-up some parts of the nose section because it knew that nature prefers round-pressure vessels, not 747-nose-shaped vessels with some flat surfaces. Despite the strengthening, cracks were detected in the forward fuselage area known as Section 41. Some cracks were found on aircraft with as few as 6,500 cycles on the log book. All 747s made before August 1987 had to be inspected and these had to be repeated regularly once 8,000 cycles had been completed.

Boeing started to use a more fatigue-resistant aluminum-copper alloy in the frames around the nose instead of the original aluminum-zinc alloy. The manufacturer also made the same changes to older 747s in service, so they required less-frequent inspections. Boeing decided to test its 747 design once again and conducted two years of pressure tests on a pair of 747s: one was a former Japan Airlines 747-100SR with the equivalent of 20,000 long-range flights on it (which was the original design lifespan of the 747); the other was a new -400 production fuselage with the redesigned Section 41. Every 1,500 cycles, the airframes were inspected closely and if any cracks were found they were monitored but not fixed. An additional 20,000 cycles were applied to the -100SR over 19 months, while the -400 was subjected to more than 40,000 cycles.

The tests produced two main results. First, they gave a much better idea of where to expect cracks in the future, thereby enabling Boeing to advise airlines on how to keep 747s flying safely much longer than the lifespan originally designed for them. Second, the tests proved that the new Section 41 design "met or exceeded" the design goals.

Although Airbus aircraft, with their circular cross-section, were less prone to fatigue problems caused by pressurization, they nonetheless had their share of problems. Early A300B2s and B4s dating from 1981 and before suffered from delamination of some joints in the fuselage. This was traced to poor preparation of some surfaces before assembly and resulted in inspections and repairs. The older A300s also required wing inspections for cracks in the rear spar after 16,700 cycles, with further inspections after 9,400 cycles.

The Lockheed TriStar also showed signs of aging in 1995 when reports suddenly came in of fatigue cracks on 20 aircraft. The Federal Aviation Administration (FAA) issued an emergency airworthiness directive calling for inspection, either externally by x-ray or internally by visual or electronic detection techniques, of all aircraft with between 20,000 and 25,000 cycles. Such was the concern that some 38 older TriStars with more than 25,000 cycles had to be checked within 25 days.

Lockheed was, however, still pleased with the TriStar's basic structural design, which had ensured no aircraft crashed due to failure by the mid-1990s. As former chief engineer Elliott Green recalled, ". . . we had a unique structural configuration because we used doublers [strengthening double-thickness parts], which were bonded on the inside of the airplane. Normally, doublers of that sort are riveted, which we thought would produce even more concentration. We designed the aircraft for a high time life and tested the structure completely on a finished aircraft. We tested it to 52,500 flights and then upped the loads by 10 percent and then another 10 percent. Eventually, we tested to 84,000 flights at higher loads in anticipation of making heavier and longer-range aircraft. In the end, it was worthwhile because the first was built with a high gross weight of 430,000 pounds and the last ones we built to 510,000 pounds."

On the Front Line

Giant jetliners tend to attract attention because they are flown by national flag-carriers all over the world as ambassadorial flagships. Unfortunately, this status, added to their very size, has also made them attractive targets for acts of violence.

The Boeing 747, due to its undisputed leadership at the high-capacity end of the market, has had more than its fair share of such encounters. Out of just over 100 significant incidents, accidents, and crashes to affect the 747 since 1969, almost 10 percent have been related to terrorism or other acts of war. One of the most infamous occurred on an August night in 1983 when a Korean Air 747-200B was shot down by a Soviet Sukhoi Su-15 fighter. Unfortunately flight 007 had wandered off course and, unknown to the crew, had penetrated Soviet airspace near the island of Sakhalin. Two AA-9 Aphid air-to-air missiles were fired at the 747; after being struck by the missiles, the 747 plunged into the sea killing all 269 aboard.

Another tragedy that caused outrage around the world was the destruction of Pan Am flight 103, a 747-100, over Lockerbie, Scotland, in December 1988. A bomb also claimed an Air India 747-200B over the Atlantic in June 1985, and another damaged a Philippine Air Lines 747-200B Combi in flight near Minami Daito Island in December 1994. At the time of this writing, the exact cause of the crash of a TWA 747-100 into the sea off Moriches Inlet, Long Island, a few minutes after takeoff from New York in July 1996 was still unclear, though terrorism and sabotage were strongly suspected.

Twin jets such as this American Airlines Boeing 767 had built up an unbeatable safety record on long-range over-water routes by the late 1990s. The increasing dominance of the twins, and particularly the 767, on trans-Atlantic and other routes led to a phenomenon called fragmentation. This basically meant that the airlines were able to offer a far wider choice of destinations with direct flights. This consequently reduced traffic on the major trunk routes, placing a question mark over the potential market size of the next-generation jumbos.

The single biggest incident of wide-body "jetocide" occurred at Kuwait International Airport during the invasion by Iraq in February 1990. Although many jets managed to escape, a British Airways 747-100 was destroyed along with two Kuwait Airways A300-620Cs and two of the same airline's 767-200ERs. By the end of 1996, war and terrorism had accounted for the destruction of one A310 in Nigeria, three A300s in the Middle East, and major damage to a fourth Air France aircraft at Houari Boumediene Airport. The first Airbus lost to a wartime event was in July 1988 near Hangam Island in the Persian Gulf when an Iran Air A300B2-200 was shot down in error by the U.S. Navy which mistook the approaching radar target for an attacking Iranian Air Force F-14.

Since 1973, it is believed that only two out of around 50 significant incidents and accidents to affect the DC-10 family have resulted from deliberate acts of violence. One of these was an amazing attack on an Ariana Afghan Airlines DC-10-30 in September 1984. As the aircraft was approaching Khwaya Ranuash airport, Kabul, from Kandahar with 321 aboard it was hit by ground fire believed to be a shoulder-launched missile. The hydraulics system, port engine, and wing were badly damaged, but the aircraft landed safely. It was later repaired and was still in service in 1997. The other incident involved a DC-10 of the French airline UTA that was destroyed in midair by a bomb over the bleak Massif de Termit region of Africa in September 1989. Another tri-jet to be lost to explosives was an Air Lanka Lockheed TriStar blown up by Tamil Tigers at Katunayake International in Sri Lanka in May 1986.

Long-Distance Twins

One of the most crucial areas of design in later generation wide-bodies has been the development of safety and backup systems for the expanding breed of long-haul twin-engined jetliners.

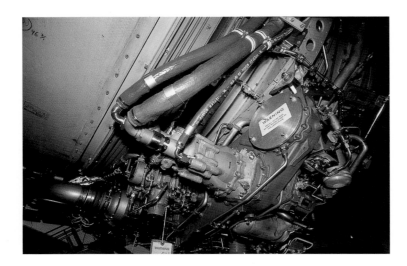

Duplication and redundancy are the key to safe operations and ETOPS. To ensure adequate backups, even the engines, like this GE CF6-80C2, drive dual hydraulic and electrical systems. Although mounted on a 747, this engine is fully interchangeable with a 767, and therefore has dual hydraulic positions. The second is hidden by the panel that is labeled "Warning."

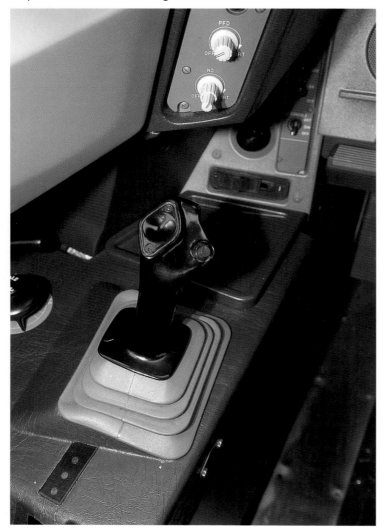

This A340 side stick controller is not mechanically connected to any flight control surface, but is instead locked to computers which interpret the pilot's control inputs.

Although some of these ETOPS routes were sometimes flown by standard-body twins such as the 757, and even the 737, the majority of long-distance, over-water routes were dominated by the Airbus A310, Boeing 767, and Boeing 777.

The long-range-twin revolution began cautiously in the mid-1980s when the first ETOPS aircraft were limited to routes that took them a maximum of 60 and then 90 minutes of flying time on one engine away from a diversionary airfield. By 1995, reliability had grown to such high levels that the 777 entered service already cleared for 180 minutes of single-engine flying time and actually flew across the Atlantic from London to Washington on its first-ever revenue-earning operation.

Every ETOPS twin was fitted with more backup systems than usual to improve the chances of either restarting a failed engine or continuing safely on the remaining powerplant. Much of the effort was focused on the electrical system, with the addition of a fourth and even fifth generator. The extra generator, or generators, was seen as a "life-support" machine for essential systems such as flight instruments, navigation, communications, cabin lighting, and the electrical signaling of flight controls, flaps, and landing gear.

Much of this backup power ultimately depended on the small APU that sits in the tail. The trouble with this location was that it was also the coldest spot on the aircraft. The APU would sit and "cold soak" for hours on end and literally freeze solid, making it very hard to start at a moment's notice, particularly at high altitude. Although improvements have gradually been made to APUs since the start of ETOPS, the ultimate design by the mid-1990s was the Allied Signal 331-500 designed for the 777. The tough early ETOPS requirements called for an APU that would start 99 percent of the time by the second attempt. The APU was, therefore, fitted with two starter motors, one electric and the other pneumatic. To warm it up, the APU was also fitted with electric bearing and gearbox heaters to stir cold, sludgy oil. The little engine was also supplied with a powerful 40-amp battery and was designed with a two-stage compressor that is easier to start than the usual single-stage unit. Further backup power is also made available from a small windmill-like device, the ram-air turbine (RAT). The RAT is hidden away in the belly of the aircraft but, in an emergency, could be dropped into the air stream, where it would spool up and instantly generate power.

Other vital systems included at least three independent hydraulic systems. The European and U.S. regulatory authorities required that ETOPS twins be able to sustain the complete loss of any two hydraulic systems plus either engine. Pneumatic systems are also important. After an engine failure, the aircraft depends on the remaining engine and APU for cabin pressurization, cabin and cockpit heating, and airframe and engine de-icing. Equipment cooling was also taken very seriously, particularly for new-generation aircraft in which the huge amount of electronics dissipates up to 14 kilovolt-amperes.

Finally, the ETOPS aircraft were designed to carry a wide array of sophisticated but highly reliable fire-detection and -suppression systems. To avoid the nightmare of in-flight fire, the aircraft carry up to 3 hours' worth of gradual-release fire-fighting bottles plus extra extinguishers for quick knockdown shots.

A computer-controlled fly-by-wire system helps protect this A340 against stalls, over speeding, and excessive loads even during dramatic maneuvers like this.

All 747 Combis, like this Swiss air-300, were fitted with improved fire fighting systems and fire-resistant materials after the loss of a South African Airways -200B Combi in the Indian Ocean in November 1987 following a cargo fire that went out of control.

One of the biggest issues facing the makers of giant jetliners of the future is infrastructure. Airbus and Boeing have toured the world's major airports to find out what is the maximum-size super-jumbo these airports could accommodate.

Airbus plans to develop the 260-foot-wingspan A3XX to challenge the mighty 747 at the top end of the market.

GIANTS OF THE TWENTY-FIRST CENTURY

THE NEXT GENERATION OF GIANT JETLINERS, AND THE biggest yet, finally began to emerge on the computer design screens and in wind tunnels in the mid-1990s. The new aircraft were truly enormous with a maximum takeoff weight of well over a million pounds and space for almost 1,000 passengers in high-density seating.

Not only were the aircraft bigger, but so was the choice. For the first time Boeing faced a challenge in the ultra-high-capacity market over which the 747 had reigned supreme for almost 30 years. After years of build-up, Airbus had decided to go ahead with a giant jetliner of its own, initially called the A3XX. The Airbus consortium took the plunge after market predictions suggested such huge aircraft would play a big part in meeting a global demand for 13,360 aircraft worth more than $1,000 billion, between 1995 and around 2014. "One-third of this will be for aircraft of more than 400 seats, where Airbus does not now compete," said spokespersons of Airbus at the time. "That is why we can't afford not to be there." In all Airbus estimated a market for 1,380 airliners with at least 500 seats worth $280 billion through 2014.

Boeing's market forecasts, on the other hand, were a lot more conservative than those of Airbus, particularly for 500 seats and above. Of this top sector, it estimated that only about 470 would be needed by 2014, roughly one-third of the Airbus forecast for that size.

The MD-XX was to be the final attempt by Douglas Aircraft to regain the market share of past years. The aircraft would have provided a perfect replacement for early 747s, as well as challenging the 777 and A340 for the long-range market. It was scrapped by McDonnell Douglas in October 1996, signaling the end of Douglas Aircraft as an independent maker of long-range jetliners.

Although Boeing had looked at stretching its 747 since the very start of the program in the 1960s, nothing had come of the studies. To begin with, the market had always been unsure, and in later years the improved 747-400 had turned out to be the best-selling version of the jumbo family to date. Boeing's attitude had been "if it isn't broken, don't fix it." Airbus, on the other hand, had been busy developing a broad family of standard-body jetliners (the A319, A320, and A321), as well as its wide-body A300, A310, A330, and A340 series and had sensibly not sought to challenge the entrenched 747 at the top end of the market. In its 26-year history, the Airbus consortium had climbed from a fragile entity offering just one airliner, the A300, to number two in the commercial jetliner business ahead of McDonnell Douglas with a 10-product family. Now, by the mid-1990s, it was suddenly in a strong position to fight it out head-to-head with Boeing in a battle of the giants.

The race to develop the new generation began slowly in 1991 when Boeing was asked by United, and later British

Airways, to study an all-new 650-seater to serve the fast-growing Asia-Pacific market. The study was based on earlier work that Boeing had done on aircraft with up to 800 seats that could ply the routes already flown by the 747-400. "We responded by working with them and began some new studies. That led us into the New Large Airplane [NLA]," said Boeing's Duane Jackson, chief engineer, product development, on what was eventually to become the 747X program. In 1992, the study gathered speed and the 600-plus-seat proposals were discussed with eight airlines, including the Asia-Pacific carriers Qantas, Singapore Airlines, ANA, and Japan Airlines, as well as British Airways, United, Lufthansa, and Air France.

Three major options emerged, two of which were based on stretched versions of the 747-400. One had seating for up to 480, while retaining the standard upper deck, and 560 if the main and upper decks were stretched with two 11.5-foot plugs fore and aft of the wing. However, both 747 derivatives were purely stopgap solutions. The only major difference, apart from the plugs in the fuselage, was the use of the stronger wing already being developed for the 747-400 freighter. The big drawback of both 747 derivatives was their range limitations. Both carried more payload than the -400 but could not go as far because they still used the same basic wing design and could not carry any more fuel.

The third option was an all-new design that Boeing offered in several variations. The baseline design was "short and fat," according to the study's chief project engineer at the time, John Roundhill, with a circular cross-section and up to 14-abreast seating in economy. Despite the onset of yet another fierce recession, Boeing's determination was not thwarted by the gloomy state of the business. Phil Condit, who was then 777 general manager, said, "If you look at our history, we always start making new aircraft in the middle of a recession, and we always start delivering them in the middle of a recovery."

While Boeing showed its "short and fat" design to its group of airlines, McDonnell Douglas was busy offering an uncannily similar design to its own selected band of loyal operators. The MD-12 was a four-engined double-decker. It was Douglas Aircraft's first serious departure from the familiar tri-jet configuration since the late 1960s. The MD-12 grew from a complex series of "almosts" and "very nearly" design studies involving stretched and "super-stretched" MD-11s. One design from 1988 even incorporated the Airbus A330 wing, but this was dropped when negotiations between Long Beach and Toulouse dried up after Airbus realized how closely the MD-11 would compete with the A330 and A340.

By 1990 the stretched MD-11 study was rewinged and redesignated the MD-12X with different family members, including a 550-seat MD-12XX. By the end of October 1991, Douglas secured board approval to offer the MD-12 to airlines, and a formal launch was expected in 1992. Then, several events conspired against Douglas. One was the growing range and payload requirements of the airlines. Some wanted capacity for 375 passengers in three classes and a range of 8,000 nautical miles. This required a much higher gross takeoff weight of 897,000 pounds, creating the need for higher-thrust engines. The inlet diameter of the more powerful engines was naturally larger, which meant that the big banjo fitting in the tri-jet's tail would have to be completely redesigned to allow more air through to the number-two engine.

Another problem was money. With airlines suffering and investors' confidence at all-time low levels, where was Douglas going to get backing for its development costs conservatively estimated at some $5 billion? The answer, it seemed, was the Taiwan Aerospace Corporation (TAC) which seemed anxious to invest in Douglas, the MD-12, and aerospace in general.

With negotiations ongoing in Taiwan and things looking pretty favorable, Douglas decided to go back to the drawing board to solve the troublesome number-two-engine intake problem. The bold answer to the dilemma was to scrap the tri-jet altogether and go for a four-engined jetliner with double decks. Douglas revealed the surprise configuration in May 1992 and, all being well, promised a first flight in 1996 and deliveries in 1997. However, all did not go well, mainly because of lack of progress in negotiations with TAC whose own investors were beginning to question the wisdom of backing the MD-12. Confusion plagued the talks. Douglas hoped to get assistance from Taiwan in raising development money, whereas TAC apparently believed that capital could be raised by the U.S. company itself using letters of credit issued by the Taiwanese government. These would be placed against $2.5 billion worth of orders for around 20 of the new jetliners which were to have been ordered by a leasing company set up by the Taiwanese government and TAC.

▲ The cost of developing a much-larger tail inlet was a contributory factor to the abandonment of the MD-XX project and, therefore, to the ultimate Boeing takeover of McDonnell Douglas.

In the end, the talks came to nothing, Douglas never found any off-shore partners. The MD-12 project was quietly shelved in 1993 and never reappeared. As recently as 1996, Douglas made a last-ditch effort to resurrect its long-term giant jetliner line by studying a revised, rewinged, and stretched MD-11. The project, known as the MD-XX, was accurately targeted at the replacement market for earlier 747s as well as competition for the 777 and A340. Swissair and other previously loyal Douglas users such as KLM and American all showed great interest, and the omens looked favorable for a time.

The company had been running a two-year campaign to restore the industry's failing faith in its long-term future, and a commitment to a new wide-body venture seemed vital. To the employees' dismay at Douglas, the board of McDonnell Douglas threw out the MD-XX plan in late October 1996 when it decided that the risk did not justify such a huge investment. With only a handful of orders left for the MD-11, most of which were for freighters, it seemed that Douglas's days in the big civil-jet business were limited. As far as giant jetliners were concerned, it seemed to have conceded to the overwhelming might of Boeing and the fast-increasing strength of Airbus. Yet, the company's impressive civil

Boeing returned briefly to the double-decker concept 25 years after rejecting it for the 747. The New Large Airplane was to have a range of 8,970 statute miles and carry more than 600 passengers in three classes. The NLA was later dropped in favor of radically modernized 747s with fuselage stretches and new wings, engines, and systems.

legacy could not be ignored. The narrow-body MD-90/95 family was still being developed, and the company was serious about selling commercial versions of the C-17 Globemaster III airlifter that had been developed for the USAF. For the future it was even looking at giant flying wing, or "blended-wing-body" aircraft.

Within days of the decision to ax the MD-XX, the previously unthinkable happened. Boeing approached McDonnell Douglas to help it design and fabricate some parts of the proposed 747-X series. Boeing was desperate for engineers and manufacturing facilities and, with the death of the MD-XX, McDonnell Douglas had both.

But that was nothing compared to what was coming next. Just weeks later, a few days after the December 8 roll-out of the Next Generation 737-700, Boeing and McDonnell Douglas agreed to merge, forming the world's largest aerospace company. It had not been a good year for McDonnell Douglas, the company having lost several major military and space contracts. The decision to terminate the MD-XX and the loss of the Joint Strike Fighter contract were the last straw, and Boeing made its move. One of the first victims of the take-over was expected to be the MD-11 which, as noted earlier, had never lived up to full sales expectations after its early performance problems. Ironically, it was the lack of airline confidence caused by the MD-11 problems which led to the cancellation of the MD-XX, and ultimately to

the Boeing take-over. The last Douglas built wide-body was therefore instrumental in the disappearance of the company.

Mergers of a different sort had been in the air in early 1993 when the saga of Boeing's NLA (New Large Airplane) took on a new twist. To the surprise of many of the airlines and the aerospace world in general, Boeing announced the start of joint studies with the four companies that form the Airbus partnership—Aerospatiale, British Aerospace, DASA, and CASA. The study looked at the feasibility of developing a multinational Very Large Commercial Transport (VLCT) and deliberately excluded Airbus itself. Many saw this as a clever gambit by Boeing to split and confuse the Airbus camp, or at least seriously delay any competing Airbus program. Instead, Boeing vehemently insisted that its intentions were strictly honorable and, given the potential size and risk of the venture, based on sound business reasoning.

The unusual group worked on how big the world market was likely to be for such a giant jetliner. It also began looking at what would actually be required to set up a joint, international company to produce the VLCT, rather than looking at any particular aircraft design in great detail. The group met alternately in Europe and the United States and, by using cleverly erected "Chinese Walls," managed to discuss details without giving any serious business secrets away. Jurgen Thomas of DASA led the European team, while John Hayhurst led the Boeing group.

Although it had only been given a year, the study was extended in 1994, and Airbus Industrie itself became involved as a kind of observer. Boeing meanwhile kept up studies of its own NLA and 747 derivatives, while Airbus continued design studies of its own A3XX, a slightly smaller 400–500-seat project that it had begun in 1992. By the end of 1994, the initial market assessment was produced showing a potential for up to 1,000 aircraft by 2020. Boeing, among others, said that this seemed insufficient market potential to warrant the enormous cost of setting up a special company to produce the VLCT.

Yet the effort continued for a while until, finally, on July 7, 1995, with the joint study by then two and a half years old, it was frozen at a meeting held on Long Island, New York. The Boeing party headed west to Seattle, and the Europeans flew home across the Atlantic. The battle of the true giants seemed imminent.

A3XX Challenge

The world's airlines, enginemakers, and Boeing waited to see what Airbus would do after the VLCT affair. They did not have to wait long. Airbus acknowledged that the study had effectively increased Boeing's lead by two years, but it responded quickly. The consortium adjusted its sights upward to a two-family A3XX series that would seat almost 1,000 passengers in its largest form. In early 1996 it established an NLA division and appointed VLCT study veteran Jurgen Thomas as its head.

Keeping in close contact with airlines, Airbus presented a major update of its studies to 13 major carriers later in 1996 in the medieval city of Carcassonne in the south of France. Representatives of the airlines were shown a huge, rather-blunt-looking aircraft with a double-deck cross-section shaped a bit like an egg. It was similar to earlier A3XX shapes produced out of its original Ultra High Capacity

▲ The design of the proposed new series of 747s started to come together in 1996. Boeing sent models to the United Kingdom's Defense Research Agency's low-speed windtunnel at Farnborough, Hampshire. Other windtunnel tests were undertaken at Seattle and in Tullahoma, Tennessee. Note the higher-bypass-ratio engines and 777-style, six-wheel bogie undercarriage.

▼ Using the A330's Trent 700 and the Boeing 777's Trent 800 as the combined base, Rolls-Royce designed a new engine called the Trent 900 for both the proposed new 747 series and the A3XX. A Trent 700 is shown here in full reverse thrust slowing down a Cathay Pacific A330 during the 1994 Farnborough air show.

Airbus planned to exploit the growth potential of both the A330 and A340 to the maximum. The higher weight and greater range of the A340-500 and -600 versions demanded an all-new engine capable of up to 60,000 pounds of thrust. This was well beyond the power capability of any further growth derivatives of the CFM56 engine, shown peeping in at the top of the picture.

A computer-generated image of the proposed A340-600. This was stretched by 20 fuselage frames over the basic A340 and was expected to carry up to 380 passengers over a range of 7,400 nautical miles. Airbus hoped the aircraft would provide a good replacement for old 747 "Classics."

Airliner (UHCA) studies, but the design was more refined and larger in concept. The "vertical ovoid" shape was the finalist from among more than 40 cross-sections and produced what Airbus called "the biggest passenger cabin in history." Although far from finalized, the seat plan provided the potential for 6-abreast in business class on the upper deck or 8-abreast for economy class. The design foresaw 10-abreast on the lower deck, with four seats in the middle aisle and three on each outside aisle. This avoided what Airbus called "prisoners" in the middle "fifth" seat on some wide-bodies.

After extensive talks with airlines and airports, Airbus decided to keep the overall length and breadth of the A3XX within a box measuring 260 x 260 feet. Any bigger than this and Airbus believed the jet would not be able to turn the corners on tighter taxiway curves at some airports. It would also be too big to maneuver at some ramps where taxiways, piers, and gates were close together.

Therefore, the wing was sized to slightly over 259.2 feet in span and was designed with an aspect ratio of around 8.0 (compared to almost 200 feet and 8.68 on the 777). The aspect ratio describes the "slenderness" of a wing and is calculated by dividing the gross area by the square of the span. In terms of the A3XX this meant the wing was broad and could cruise easily for long distances and store huge quantities of fuel. The initial A3XX-100 version, at this stage, was designed for a range of 7,450 nautical miles with 555 passengers in three classes. By late 1996 slightly more range was added for the baseline model

to give it "legs" for another 50 or 60 nautical miles and the maximum gross takeoff weight had climbed more than 65,000 pounds to 1,124,000 pounds.

Airbus quickly saw the need for a longer-range -100R as an early member of the family. The -100R was designed to fly around 1,000 nautical miles farther with the same passenger load. Maximum takeoff weight was revised upward to 1,212,000 pounds as a result. The same weight was also defined for the stretched A3XX-200 which could carry almost 660 passengers in three classes. In an all-economy layout, the -200 would be capable of taking a staggering 1,000 people! Maximum payload for both -100 versions was set at around 187,000 pounds, whereas the larger -200 was aimed at 209,000 pounds. Maximum fuel capacity for all three was a whopping 705,000 pounds, thanks mainly to the huge wing.

Airbus estimated that its A3XX series would cruise at around Mach 0.85, "plus some flexibility," it added. The lumbering monster would take 200 nautical miles, or around 30 minutes, to reach an initial cruise altitude of 33,000 feet in the case of the -200, or 35,000 feet in the case of the -100. Take-off-field length at sea level was expected to be 11,000 feet, while approach speed was close to that of the 747 growth models: at or below 150 knots.

Fuselage length was set at 232.3 feet for the shorter -100, while the larger -200 still undercut the original "box" by 6 feet, being 254 feet long. The overall height was expected to be almost 80 feet, mainly because of the shorter, stocky shape of the fuselage and the requirement for good lateral control. The overall height of the body was designed to be almost 28 feet high, compared to almost 26 feet for the 747. Fuselage width was 22.8 feet externally, with an internal width of 21.4 feet. Airbus believed one of its major advantages over the 747 was that the ovoid shape allowed both the upper and main decks to have twin aisles. The 747 had only two aisles on the main deck and a single aisle on the upper deck. The A3XX was also designed with dual-lane stairs connecting the two decks, which played a big part in an estimated turnaround time of between 70 and 95 minutes for the -100, compared with its projections of more than 120 minutes for the new 747s.

The entire Airbus project was driven by the need to undercut the direct operating costs of the 747, and particularly the proposed next generation -500X and -600X models. By mid-1996, Airbus said the A3XX-100 would have 17 percent lower seat-mile costs than the 747-400, while the larger -200 would be around 23 percent lower. By raising the range and payload abilities slightly in later versions, Airbus hoped to keep an edge over Boeing. Airbus believed its biggest playing card was the clean-sheet design of the A3XX, whereas the 747 growth models suffered the inevitable penalty of being derived from a 30-year-old design.

New 747s

Boeing had looked at stretching the 747 since the very start of the program in the late 1960s. It had also considered a more fundamental change of wing several times. In the 1970s, these possibilities leaned more toward increasing the span of the existing wing with root plugs or tip extensions, rather than an all-new wing. In the early 1980s, the study was revisited as Boeing

▲ Boeing's answer to the 747 "Classic" replacement market was the 777-300. This was stretched with a 10-frame (17.5-foot) plug forward of the wing and a 9 frame (15.7-foot) plug added aft. The first 777-300, seating up to 369 in a typical three-class layout, was due to be delivered in May 1998 to Cathay Pacific. Launched at the 1995 Paris air show, the -300 was displayed in model form at the 1996 Farnborough air show.

▲ As giant jetliners got longer, so did the risk of tail scrape. This was a serious worry as the aircraft could sustain considerable damage to the sensitive area near the aft pressure bulkhead if the tail area was scraped along the runway during takeoff. This retractable tail-skid was pictured beneath the fin of a brand-new Qantas 767-300ER. Similar devices are planned for the 757-300 and 777-300.

The demand for super-jumbos has been diluted by the widespread use of large twin jets on long over-water routes. This process, called fragmentation, is increasing with the introduction of even larger twins such this 777-200. This aircraft, G-ZZZB, was the GE90-powered ETOPS testbed in 1996.

searched for ways to extend the range and payload for what was to become the 747-400.

Boeing juggled its options, which included a new wing-to-body fairing, winglets, or a 9 foot tip extension. The cost of these modifications was relatively small and offered a valuable 2 percent reduction in fuel consumption. A new wing, on the other hand, offered a very attractive 9 percent fuel reduction, but would have cost vastly more to develop. In 1984, as a result of its studies, Boeing outlined a "new wing measuring 240 feet to 260 feet in span for potential introduction in the late 1990s," said marketing brochures at the time. In the meantime, it opted for the cheaper solution to getting more range out of the 747 which was otherwise externally identical to the earlier 747-300.

A decade later, as the market research from the VLCT study began to come together, Boeing knew the omens again favored a stretched, rewinged 747, rather than an NLA. According to John Hayhurst, "The 747 gave us a different perspective on what the airlines really wanted. That caused us to readdress the issue. We worked out that there certainly was not a sufficient market for an all-new airplane with more than 600 seats. That alone caused us to look at something smaller and a lot less costly in 1995." Another reason was the projected development cost of the super-jumbo. Boeing Commercial Airplane Group president Ron Woodard said,

"We estimated the non-recurring cost to be anywhere from $12 billion to $15 billion. We concluded that there simply wasn't a large enough market to justify that sort of investment."

The airlines themselves also had a say. Most, if not all, of the airlines in the market for the next-generation jumbo were already 747 operators. The prospect of family commonality with a new generation of 747 suddenly began to seem more attractive against the background of spiraling costs and falling revenues. Another equally vital incentive for Boeing to opt for a 747-based super-jumbo and not an NLA was time. Some airlines, such as British Airways and Singapore Airlines, made it obvious as early as 1995 that they would buy a super-jumbo there and then if it were available. Whatever design was first to the market would undoubtedly hold the advantage, at least for the first five years or so of the competition. By going to the 747 option, Boeing could realistically aim at getting the first aircraft built, tested, certified, and delivered by December 2000, some three years ahead of the A3XX.

The original airline working group of 12 airlines that initially helped Boeing with the outline design of the NLA moved onto the 747 "rewing" or 747-X studies, and their ranks swelled to 19 airlines. "Eventually it became obvious that from cost and market considerations the 747-X was the winner," said Duane Jackson. "It was something we could afford to build and the airlines could afford to buy."

At first, Boeing tried to steer the new 747 derivatives toward as simple an approach as possible, with maximum commonality between the -400 and two larger versions that were dubbed the -500X and -600X. (Boeing denotes all proposed aircraft with an X until formally launched.) Then, the airlines themselves began to put

▲ Even a model gives some idea as to the huge size of the 747-600X compared to the standard -400.

The ambitious long-range, high-payload performance of both versions depended on the same big wing. Closely resembling a 777 wing, scaled up by around 40 percent, the new airfoil reached a span of around 255 feet, compared to 211 feet on the -400 or 195 feet for the first 747s. The wing was also less highly swept, with an angle of around 36 degrees (compared to 37.5 on the baseline 747 or just over 31 for the 777). It was also fitted with single-slotted flaps rather than the mechanically complex triple-slotted units on the 747. This was aimed at improving reliability and, more important, reducing the noise made by the airframe. The leading edge was designed with rigid Krueger flaps inboard and variable-camber Kruegers outboard. The area was increased enormously from 5,500 square feet to 8,100 square feet.

The -600X fuselage was increased in length with a 23-foot body extension to the forward section and a 21.5-foot stretch to the aft body section, taking overall length to 277 feet, 5 inches. This made it 2 feet longer than the mighty six-engined Antonov An-225, which had easily been the largest aircraft in the world up to that point and the first to ever fly with a gross weight of more than a million pounds. The -500X was reduced in length to around 250 feet overall, which still made it almost 20 feet longer than the basic 747. Boeing decided to reduce the -500X length by about nine feet between April and July 1996 in order to trade weight for range. As a result, the -500X range went up from 8,150 nautical miles to 8,700 nautical miles, but its passenger capacity fell by around 25 to 462. The final dimensions of the two giants were close to becoming frozen by the end of 1996 when detailed wind-tunnel tests were completed at the United Kingdom's Defence Research Agency's test site in Farnborough, Hampshire.

The huge "tail feathers" of the new 747 were also replaced with a new, 777-like horizontal tail that was 71 feet high, replacing the low-aspect-ratio design of the 1960s. The more pointed vertical fin was fitted with a split, double-hinged rudder for better low-speed control. A new horizontal tail was also designed with split, double-hinged elevators. The huge tail spanned almost 85 feet, just 9 feet short of the wingspan of the 737-200!

Other changes included the addition of a retractable tail skid like that used on the stretched 777, 767, and 757; a new wing-to-body fairing; and the use of the 777-style six-wheeled main undercarriage on the outer legs. The outer wheel base measured around 35 feet. The inner set retained the same 4-wheel design as on the original 747, which meant that the aircraft had a total of 20 main wheels, compared to the original's 16. To help spread the weight, which was expected to be just under 1.2 million pounds, even the nose leg was fitted with four parallel wheels in a similar way to those on the Lockheed Martin Galaxy, giving the new 747 a grand total of 24 wheels. (In this respect the An-225 was still ahead with an awesome array of 32 wheels!)

New Engines

The enginemakers hoped to offer slightly modified versions of existing 777 or A330 engines for the new super-jumbo projects. As both airframe manufacturers got closer to defining final designs, it became more obvious that new or heavily modified engines would be needed. The existing engines were either too heavy and power-

pressure on Boeing to be more aggressive with new technology for the derivatives despite the fact that these more ambitious and complicated designs could take longer to develop. As one member of the United Air Lines advisory group said, "Most of the airlines wanted new stuff like fly-by-wire because they did not want to take delivery of a new airplane in 2000 with 20-year-old technology."

Boeing had already decided to use major technologies developed for the 777, such as the wing, six-wheel main undercarriage, and some systems on the new 747s. Boeing then took the whole process even further to include fly-by-wire flight-control technology and new avionics, flight-deck displays, and interior architecture. "The change to 777-based systems probably helped because it is state-of-the-art and the team is mostly still here, so to take that architecture and put it in the 747 is probably an easier task than updating the 747-400," said John Hayhurst in late 1996. Duane Jackson added that "We made a lot of changes in systems to take advantage of 777 developments. We combined that with a system architecture for four-engines [not two, like on the 777], and the cross-section of the 747. We've captured what is appropriate from both families."

With airlines clamoring for higher capacity, Boeing expected to launch the larger 747-600X first. By late 1996 this was defined with seats for around 538 in three classes, compared to 416 on the 747-400. It would have a design range of 7,750 nautical miles "to ensure with confidence that it will be able to fly the same missions as the -400," said Jackson. The extra seating generated a 10-percent improvement in operating cost terms (measured in dollars per seat mile) over the -400. "On the same basis we'd hold our own and even show a modest improvement with the smaller -500X while increasing its range," added Jackson. The -500X was designed to be a shorter version of the -600X rather than a stretch of the -400. It would carry around 460 passengers on longer routes up to 8,700 nautical miles. This enabled it to fly from Dallas/Fort Worth, Texas, directly to Hong Kong, or from Los Angeles, California, to Singapore. The -500X was also designed to offer more cargo capacity on routes at the payload limit of the -400's capabilities in the mid-1990s, such as Los Angeles to Sydney, Australia. The -600X was aimed at "classic 400 routes," such as San Francisco to Hong Kong, or Singapore to London.

Russia's next giant jetliner to enter service will be the Il-96M, which finally received a production go-ahead order in late 1996. The P&W-powered prototype is pictured here at the 1994 Farnborough air show.

ful or too small for the final needs of either Airbus or Boeing. Some, such as the Trent 800 engine developed for the 777, could be tailored to fit quite closely, but the result would still have been a compromise. Boeing had specified a target of reducing seat-mile costs by 10 percent, and the enginemakers realized that 777-derivative engines would make this very difficult to achieve.

This was a disappointment to all the enginemakers, who desperately wanted new applications for their new-generation engines which had cost a fortune to develop and yet were hard to make money on. Everyone reluctantly went back to the drawing board to study new options. Then, at the Asian Aerospace show, the first seeds of a partnership were sown between GE and P&W, when the two companies had brief, informal contact. Encouraged by Boeing, the two enginemakers continued exploratory talks, and on May 8, 1996, announced the signing of an agreement to jointly develop a new jet engine for the 747-500X and -600X.

The agreement caught much of the aerospace world off guard and appeared to leave Rolls-Royce firmly out in the cold. The British company, far from reacting gloomily, was quite pleased. For the first time in any major wide-body contest the UK enginemaker said the GE-P&W joint venture would allow it to compete for a full 50 percent of the market rather than squabble over thirds, as usual. In addition, it felt comfortable that for the first time since the advent of the big fan engine it

was well placed to offer the most attractive engine first. The Trent 800 had turned out to be the lightest engine of the three options on the 777, proving to the manufacturer that its three-shaft design was at last paying dividends in this new high-thrust bracket. Rolls-Royce banked on the successful architecture of the Trent 800 plus some features of the 700 to produce the Trent 900 with a takeoff thrust of around 77,000 pounds with growth capability to 85,000 pounds. The engine used a lighter version of the 9-foot, 2-inch diameter Trent 800 fan. The Trent 900 also used a scaled-down version of the Trent 895 intermediate- and high-pressure compressors but included new turbine blades.

Details of the newly christened GE-P&W Engine Alliance were finally revealed at the 1996 Farnborough air show when the two enginemakers unveiled the GP7176, the first member of the GP7000 family. "Both companies believe that a derivative engine will not fully meet the fuel burn, operating economies, noise, and payload/range requirements of the Boeing 747 growth aircraft," said a joint statement. The two divided up responsibility for the engine with GE taking the high-pressure compressor and turbine and combustor and P&W developing the fan and low-pressure compressor and turbine. The Alliance knew that it needed to boost performance of the engine to meet, or beat, the promises being made by Rolls-Royce. After much debate, the GP7176 was developed with the same size fan as the Trent 900, but only after a late decision to move it up in size by 2 inches. The fan was made with lightweight, hollow titanium blades, as on the PW4084, rather than the composite blades of the giant GE90 engine.

Both new engines were tied closely to the tight 747X time scale, which meant making first runs in 1998 and achieving certification in late 1999. By late 1996, both groups were also aligning themselves with the A3XX project, and in November Rolls-Royce and Airbus signed a memorandum of understanding covering the use of the Trent 900 on the European super-jumbo. Apart from the partial Rolls-Royce involvement in the IAE-powered Airbus narrow-body family, the agreement marked only the second time that the UK enginemaker had been associated with an Airbus wide-body. Jurgen Thomas noted that ". . . we are building on the cooperation started with the Trent 700, currently equipping the A330. This venture further reinforces the European aircraft industry and significantly advances the A3XX project."

Death Of A Dream

While Airbus began to accelerate its A3XX plans, Boeing was finding it increasingly hard to sell its 747-500X and -600X. There were several reasons, not least of which was the A3XX itself. On paper, the all-new Airbus design offered attractive operating costs compared to the 747X. Another reason was the price. Airlines were reeling from "sticker shock" at the proposed $200 million plus price tag of the new 747. Many of the most likely launch customers had held out for introductory incentive prices, but all had been disappointed.

The huge cost was connected to the spiraling development expenses. Originally estimated at between $1 billion and $2 billion, the costs had grown daily as the derivatives became more sophisticated. As airlines demanded more high-tech 777 features, such as fly-by-wire, the cost rose and by the end development was estimated at $7 billion.

Boeing hoped to announce the launch of the new 747s at the 1996 Farnborough air show. However, by September it still had no firm orders, and apart from a handful of commitments from Thai Airways International and Malaysian Airlines, began to see interest waning. It reluctantly slipped the launch date until the end of the year but remained confident about the program.

By December the outlook for the 747-X pair had become even gloomier. Senior Boeing officials began publicly back-pedaling on the 747-X. At the December roll out of the 737-700, Boeing president Phil Condit said the odds on a firm go-ahead had reduced to "around 50/50." Meanwhile the detailed design work was well underway with more than 1,000 staff on the project and expenditure rising to around $1 million per day. Something had to give. Finally, on January 20, 1997, Boeing released the shock news that it was shelving the 747-500X and -600X and concentrating instead on the development of the 767-400ERX and 777-200X and -300X long range twins. Many of the airlines were taken completely by surprise, as were the enginemakers which were busy defining designs and briefing airlines at the time of the announcement.

Boeing's decision hinged on several factors, the most vital being lack of customers and market size. The airlines' total apathy to the 747-X added weight to the company's own detailed analysis that continued to show the potential market for the 500-plus seater was shrinking, not growing. One of the main reasons for this was the bounding success of the long range twinjets that had enabled the development of many point-to-point routes which bypassed the traditional trunk routes. Boeing predicted this "fragmentation" effect would continue, further eroding the super jumbo marketplace.

▲ Land of the giants. Congestion, booming passenger numbers, and surging economies make Asia the powerhouse behind the demand for bigger and bigger jetliners. A typical day at Hong Kong's Kai Tak airport shows the usual array of giant jetliners with only a handful of narrow-bodies in evidence.

The company's decision came at a time of unparalleled activity for Boeing. The take-over of Rockwell was underway and the $13.3 billion acquisition of McDonnell Douglas had just been announced. The commercial jetliner business was booming with more than 700 new orders taken in 1996, and the defense side of the company was enjoying one of its best ever periods winning both the Joint Strike Fighter downselect and the 747-based airborne laser contracts. Boeing was being stretched in every direction, and the release of funds and personnel from the 747-X project was considered the best use of its thinly spread resources.

For the moment at least, Boeing appeared to be handing the initiative to Airbus. Boeing blew the dust off earlier studies of an increased gross weight 747-400 and a simpler stretch that could seat an extra 80 passengers but brushed off any suggestions of plans to develop either the re-winged 747 or an NLA.

To prepare itself for the challenge, Airbus began forming itself into a formal company, as opposed to a consortium, in order to be able to attract major new investment to back the super-jumbo and other projects. By mid-1997, Airbus remained committed to the A3XX and aimed to complete preliminary design freeze by the end of the year with authority to offer the aircraft in 1998. Formal launch was anticipated in late 1999. Entry into service was planned for late 2003, some two years after Boeing's target for the 747-X. Airbus said airports welcomed the delay as it gave them two extra years to get ready for the new monster. To help share the risk, Airbus began wooing new international partners outside the existing Airbus family, including several in the United States, among them big names such as Lockheed Martin.

The Europeans remained confident that they would tap a market estimated in 1997 at 1,383 aircraft worth $276 billion. Boeing continued to scoff at Airbus's market claims, saying that to equal that projection the world's top 25 747 users would each have to buy 56 big 600 seaters. One Boeing forecaster said Airbus must be "suicidal" to enter the high capacity market. Airbus countered

▲ Although this An-225 does not carry passengers, its enormous bulk is representative of the giant jetliners of the future. Any ground handling problem suffered by this leviathan is a lesson for Airbus and Boeing. The six-engined An-225 is the only one ever built. The unusual bumps on top of the fuselage are coverings for attachments that were designed to secure the Buran in position. The Buran was Russia's answer to the U.S. Space Shuttle but was scrubbed for financial reasons.

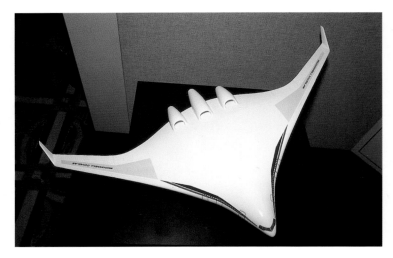

▲ The last-ever new project made public before McDonnell Douglas was bought by Boeing was the Blended Wing Body (BWB-1-1). Powered by three engines in typical Douglas style, the flying wing was designed to carry up to 800 passengers across 7,000 nautical miles. Wingspan with winglets was estimated at around 289 feet.

saying the A3XX would provide the next logical giant jetliner after the 747, despite the fragmentation effect. Airbus conceded that fragmentation existed; after all, its own A300/A310 and A330/A340 models had contributed substantially to the process. It argued, however, that the sheer growth in overall traffic, plus the airline's continuing need to make profits, meant there would be room for both consolidation and fragmentation. In other words, the market would exist for both the A3XX and all the new big twins.

Near-Term Giants

While the titanic struggle of the super-jumbos hogged the limelight in 1996 and 1997, a whole series of new giant twin derivatives was quietly emerging from Airbus and Boeing. In the case of Boeing, these twins were largely responsible for the sudden termination of the 747X. The largest, in terms of length, was the 777-300. This was a stretched version of the standard -200 and, at just over 242 feet, was the longest jetliner ever built. Although a few feet short of the mighty Antonov An-224 and Lockheed Martin C-5, the -300 was longer than the 747 and 10 feet longer than the proposed A3XX-100. Only the 254 foot long A3XX-200 was expected to eclipse it in the early part of the twenty-first century. Boeing launched the giant jetliner at the 1995 Paris show with commitments for 31 aircraft.

The 777 was Boeing's "jet for all seasons," and the -300 was just one of several versions of the big twin planned to meet the various needs of the airlines. The baseline 777-200 formed a good replacement for DC-10s and L-1011s on trans-continental or transatlantic routes, while the increased gross weight (IGW) version offered the same capacity on much longer routes such as London to Los Angeles. The stretched -300 was aimed at the emerging replacement market for aging 747-100s and -200s as it could seat 368 in three classes, or 451 in a two-class arrangement. The first of these giants, which incorporated a 17-foot, 6-inch stretch ahead of the wing and a 15-foot, 8-inch stretch behind the wing, was set to be delivered to Cathay Pacific in May 1998.

The sheer length of the -300 demanded several new innovations, including a TV camera system used by the crew to help them taxi and turn corners. The aircraft was fitted with two cameras in the tail that look forward to show the main gear, and another camera under the belly that shows the nose wheels. The picture is displayed on a screen in the flight deck.

In early 1997, Boeing completed the family by offering airlines two new versions, dubbed the -200X and -300X. The -200X was designed to fly longer routes than any airliner in history, including the 747-400. With seating for almost 300 passengers, the heavyweight twin was designed with a take-off weight of around 720,000 pounds, giving it a range of 8,600 nautical miles. This enabled it to fly from Singapore to Los Angeles without any refueling stops. Boeing marketeers openly admitted the flights would be long, up to 18 hours, but claimed this was still better than the one stop alternative. "You get on, read 'War and Peace' and get off. But it's still better than having to stop in Tokyo or Taipei!" said one marketing specialist. The heavyweight -300X was designed with a maximum take-off weight of just over 700,000 pounds that enabled it to carry around 350 passengers on even the longest routes flown by 747-200s. With only two engines, instead of the four on the 747, Boeing expected the -300X's operating costs to be up to 25 percent lower.

The other projected new twin in the Boeing pantheon was the long-awaited 767-400ERX stretch. First proposed as one of the early study options that eventually emerged as the 777, the stretched 767 was able to carry up to 40 more passengers on long range routes such as Europe to the West Coast of America. The stretch was also furnished with winglets and other aerodynamic improvements and was launched in 1997 with orders and options for 70 aircraft.

Airbus, like Boeing, did not neglect its other wide-bodies during the intensive buildup to the super-jumbos. After years of design studies, in April 1996, Airbus finally announced plans to develop a "super-stretch" derivative of the four-engined A340. The consortium hoped

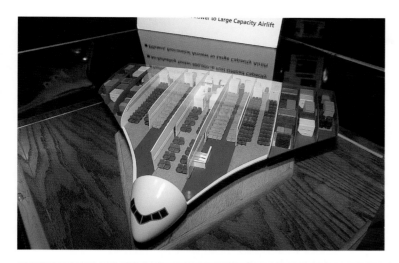

The BWB-1-1 design used the basic wing structure to provide compartments for passengers and freight. A second deck is located below.

Boeing's decision to shelve its 747 stretch plans in January 1997 had a lot to do with this aircraft, the proposed 767-400ERX. Stretched by 21 feet, this was one of a new breed of giant twinjets which Boeing believed would come to dominate the market in the twenty-first century. The company decided it was better to invest in the new 767, and its long range stable mates the 777-200X and -300X, rather than pour $7 billion into the re-winged 747-500X and -600X. First deliveries of the 767-400 are scheduled for 2000.

to do with the A340 what Douglas had achieved 30 years earlier with the "Super Sixty" DC-8 family. The basis of the new development was a larger wing and more powerful engines. By combining these new features with a stretched fuselage, the A340-600, as it was called, could attain higher capacity and longer range. Alternatively, much longer range could also be achieved using the new wing and engines but a fuselage of the same size as the A340-300's on another version, the A340-500. At one stage, Airbus also considered a simple stretch of the A340 called the -400, but this was later dropped to focus on the more marketable rewinged and re-engined versions.

The new wing used the same front and rear spars of the existing A340 wing but had a 600-square-foot increase in area, thanks to a larger span of almost 210 feet and a larger chord. The bigger wing also held up to 25 percent more fuel and kept the winglets of the basic version. Fuselage length of the "Super Stretch" went up to around 245 feet, or slightly longer than the 777-300 stretch. To improve control of the long-body jetliner in the pitch (up and down) mode, Airbus considered using canards, or small winglike surfaces near the nose. The canards, which are used on fighter aircraft such as the Eurofighter EF2000 and Saab JAS-37 Gripen, were tested in a wind tunnel but later rejected. Airbus studied putting up to 22 extra fuselage frames in the body, 3 of which were in a new center-

body section over the new wing. The same center-body section was also to be used in the longer-range -500 that Airbus expected to be able to fly up to 8,500 nautical miles with a cargo of more than 300 passengers. This was almost 550 nautical miles farther than the smaller A340-8000 that Airbus had developed as a super long-range version of the -200 in the mid-1990s.

The same new center section was also considered for a "Super Stretch" A330 twin, known as the A330-600, powered by Boeing 777 types of engines. This was to be a stablemate to a potential 12-frame stretch also being considered. The A330-400, as it was called, was designed to carry 380 passengers over distances of almost 3,800 nautical miles.

Far Horizons

Forecasting by its very nature is highly uncertain. As Boeing president Phil Condit said in October 1996, "When you attempt to look far into the future, one thing you can predict with accuracy is that all your predictions will be wrong—either too bold or far too conservative. In the next 20 years, there may well be advances in commercial aircraft design and manufacturing—in product and process improvement—that will literally astound us."

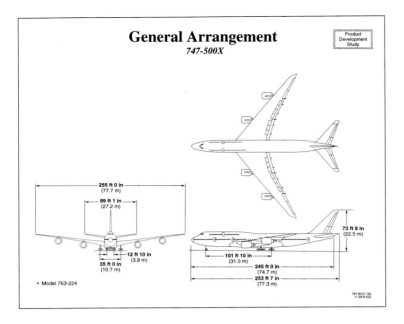

General Arrangement
747-500X

Product
Development
Study

255 ft 0 in
(77.7 m)

89 ft 1 in
(27.2 m)

73 ft 8 in
(22.5 m)

12 ft 10 in
(3.9 m)

35 ft 0 in
(10.7 m)

101 ft 10 in
(31.0 m)

245 ft 0 in
(74.7 m)

253 ft 7 in
(77.3 m)

• Model 763-224

797-6CO-132
11-25-6-GG

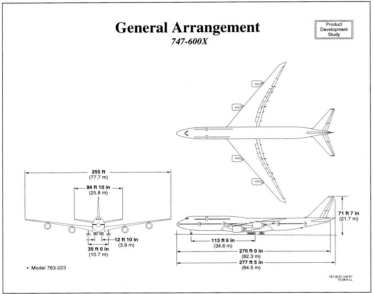

General Arrangement
747-600X

Product
Development
Study

255 ft
(77.7 m)

84 ft 10 in
(25.8 m)

71 ft 7 in
(21.7 m)

12 ft 10 in
(3.9 m)

35 ft 0 in
(10.7 m)

113 ft 6 in
(34.6 m)

270 ft 0 in
(82.3 m)

277 ft 5 in
(84.5 m)

• Model 763-223

797-6CO-104 R1
10-28-6-LL

Most forecasters agreed that passenger growth is highly likely to double to more than 2.8 billion per year by 2006 and continue to boom beyond that. The need for giant jetliners was, therefore, viewed as a certainty, but one of the main unknowns was how many super-jumbos would be needed. The relatively simple relationship between greater numbers and bigger planes no longer applied because of the effects of fragmentation. Even Boeing, a devout believer in fragmentation, kept its options open with a design for a future 650 seater, the 747-700X.

The aircraft was effectively Boeing's NLA reborn, with a new diameter 747-look-alike fuselage. The -700X used the new wing, systems, and engines of the 747-500X and -600X as a foundation. In this way, Boeing sought to reassure its customers that it had plans to meet the 650-passenger-size market for the future and, at the same time, cut down on development costs by taking this "building block" approach. At the time of the announcement, Boeing Commercial president Ron Woodard said the "rebodied" 747-600X would enable the company to meet the demand "should a sufficient market eventually develop 10 to 15 years from now. I want to make it clear, however, that we do not see a market requirement that would permit a financially viable airplane program for an airplane this size."

The monster -700X, at the time, was expected to be around 279 feet in length, with a wingspan of 253 feet, and a 75-foot-high tail. Fundamentally, however, it looked just like a very big 747. Other companies were looking at some very different designs for the longer-term future, among them Airbus, McDonnell Douglas, and even Lockheed Martin. Airbus, for instance, in its UHCA studies of a 600- to 800-seater, had looked at joining two A340 fuselages laterally to create an oval fuselage 260 feet long with a wingspan of almost 256 feet. Later versions were depicted with horizontal double-bubble, ovoid, circular, and even cloverleaf cross-sections.

Some companies examined interiors of such future aircraft in a very different way. An interior specialist company, Ogle Design, came up with the Air Cruiser concept, which offered comfort levels more reminiscent of a cruise liner than an aircraft. Instead of the usual method of entering through narrow cabin doors, passengers boarded through an 8-foot-wide nose door that hinged upward. The passengers were greeted at a reception desk which became a bar in flight and were directed to seating on two levels. The spacious aircraft contained a large area at the aft end of the lower deck for a games room and bar and on the upper deck for a restaurant. The business-class area was also provided with a business lounge. In some ways, the Air Cruiser concept was a step back in time to the early days of the 747 when interior designers planned onboard amenities ranging from piano bars and lounges to mini-cinemas. This, in turn, had been an attempt to recreate the lost grandeur of earlier airships such as the *Hindenburg*, the spacious Short Brothers Empire flying boats, or the Boeing Stratocruiser. In the end, all such luxuries were made impossible by the fuel crisis of the early 1970s and the need, ever after, to put as many fare-paying people as possible in the space available. Future planners hope the operating economics of the new designs will allow comfort and profit to coexist in the same airframe.

Airbus, McDonnell Douglas, and Lockheed Martin were all studying various flying-wing concepts in the 1990s. The Airbus studies, conducted in association with Russian aerospace companies and academies, looked at a tailless design that resembled the Northrop Grumman B-2 stealth bomber. The 340-foot-span aircraft could seat up to 900 on two decks. The FW-900, as it was called, had a maximum takeoff weight of almost 1.3 million pounds and was powered by three 120,000-pound-thrust engines mounted above the rear fuselage.

McDonnell Douglas's Blended-Wing-Body (BWB-1-1) design was shown publicly in late 1996 and was expected to be tested in scale-model form in conjunction with NASA and Stanford University the next year. Like the FW-900, the BWB-1-1 had double-deck seating for more than 800. Passengers were seated in conventional cabinlike sections that were formed from the major structural cells of the aircraft, which had a wingspan of almost 290 feet, including large winglets. The company believed that the superior aerodynamic capabilities of the shape would allow the use of three relatively small 50,000-pound-thrust-class engines. The resulting economics looked very promising, with a fuel burn almost 30 percent lower than a conventional equivalent. The BWB-1-1 concept was pursued by Boeing following its takeover of McDonnell Douglas, and plans were made in 1997 to build a piloted, sub-scale flying demonstrator to test at Edwards AFB, California.

While high-capacity airliners were still expected to rule the air routes of the future, the long-held dream of a giant supersonic jetliner was taking shape in the mid-1990s. The next-generation SST was

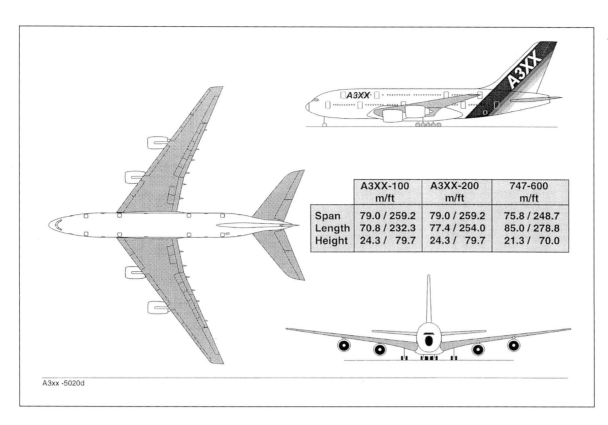

Airbus planned to freeze the final design of the A3XX by the end of 1998, though it is expected to be broadly similiar to the arrangement shown here.

	A3XX-100 m/ft	A3XX-200 m/ft	747-600 m/ft
Span	79.0 / 259.2	79.0 / 259.2	75.8 / 248.7
Length	70.8 / 232.3	77.4 / 254.0	85.0 / 278.8
Height	24.3 / 79.7	24.3 / 79.7	21.3 / 70.0

A3xx -5020d

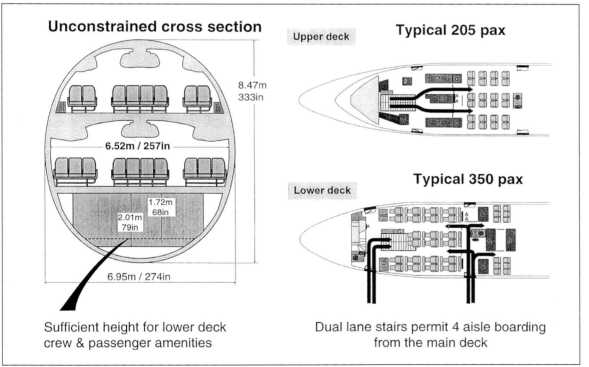

Unconstrained cross section

8.47m 333in

6.52m / 257in

1.72m 68in

2.01m 79in

6.95m / 274in

Sufficient height for lower deck crew & passenger amenities

Upper deck

Typical 205 pax

Lower deck

Typical 350 pax

Dual lane stairs permit 4 aisle boarding from the main deck

being designed as an economic and environmentally friendly follow-up to the Anglo-French Concorde. The effort was focused through NASA's High Speed Research (HSR) program which basically concentrated the best of U.S. industry and research together in one effort. The HSR effort was divided into phases with HSR I beginning in 1989, looking at the key environmental issues such as noise and pollution. HSR II began in the mid-1990s studying key technologies required to make an environmentally acceptable high-speed civil transport (HSCT).

The new HSCT is designed to carry around three times as many passengers as the Concorde and fly twice as far. The 300-plus-seater would fly at least 5,000 nautical miles at Mach 2.4, cutting by more than half the journey time from New York to Paris. Alternatively, it would cut the average time for the journey from Los Angeles to Tokyo to 4.3 hours, compared to 10.3 hours today. Boeing and McDonnell Douglas led an industry-academic team to study airframe technologies, while GE and P&W formed a similar team to study engine technologies.

The first commercial HSCT operations are not expected to begin much before 2020—a full 50 years after Pan Am introduced the first 747 into service. Ironically, many airlines at that time, including Pan Am, believed that the reign of the giant jetliner would be cut short by the advent of SSTs. How wrong they were! Using history as a guide to the future, possibly the only firm prediction to be made for the next century is that giant jetliners will continue to grow in numbers and in size.

INDEX